CHOCOLATE

Jan Hedh
Klas Andersson

BARNES
& NOBLE

NEW YORK

Page 1: Chocolate Truffle, p. 51.

Page 2: Dipping preserved cherries in chocolate, p. 58.

Page 3: Parrot made of blown caramel. Blown caramel is another of the author's specialties. The recipe is not in this book however.

Page 4: Passion Fruit and Chocolate Bavaroise, with fresh berries encased in white chocolate, p 154.

Page 5: Chocolate sculpture, made with gelatin molds, p. 37.

Page 6: Molding Santa Claus.

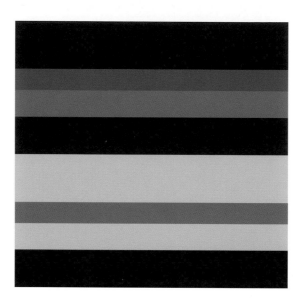

Copyright © 2002 by Jan Hedh
Photographs copyright© 2002 by Klas Andersson
Graphic design: Magdalena and Magnus Günther, BIGG
Translation: Martin Heap

This edition published by Barnes & Noble, Inc.,
by arrangement with Bokförlaget Prisma

2005 Barnes & Noble Books

ISBN 0-7607-7419-6

Printed and bound in China

05 06 07 08 09 M 9 8 7 6 5 4 3 2 1

Contents

Introduction

Cycling round our childhood Malmö, the smell of roasted cocoa beans would often entice us boys to Mazetti's chocolate factory on Bergsgatan. Chocolate candy rejects were sold behind the factory, making it a strong competitor to the school canteen. Palla's candy store was another often-visited favorite. Malmö had many small chocolate makers in those days and many bakers made their own chocolates. Chocolate-dipped orange peel was a favorite buy at Fridhem's cake shop. We ate cream buns dipped in thick chocolate at Braun's tearooms on Gustav Adolf Square. They had three more branches, ensuring that we were never without these delicacies. Malmö's proximity to Copenhagen meant that I went on many "tours" there with my parents to buy cheap groceries in the 50s and 60s. Swiss chocolate, such as Toblerone or Ragusa, were the highlights of the trip.

My introduction to chocolate-making began during my first Christmas as an apprentice at Heidi in Limhamn. My boss, Filip Liljekvist, dipped the candies and I decorated them with walnuts and suchlike, before packing them in gold boxes with the firm's name on the front. I can still remember how good the whole bakery smelt.

Then I began work at Blekingsborg's patisserie in Malmö. Kurt Lundgren was foreman there and he was a confectionary expert—French nougat, Russian jam, cream buns and ice chocolate being among his specialties. Swedish chocolate candies were quite plain and simple in those days and did not bear comparison with Continental confectionaries, but today we have a couple of chocolate makers of international class here in Sweden.

My interest in chocolate was really awakened at the Coba School in Basel, where we were taught to make all kinds of chocolates. I would come home from school with large boxes full of chocolate candies, much to the delight of my mother and sisters. Later, during my time at Conditori Hollandia bakery in Malmö we made many chocolate candies and Easter eggs. Easter and Christmas were the big chocolate festivals, clearly reflected in our fantastic window displays. My subsequent period at Conditori Lundagård bakery was also filled with chocolate from morning to night.

The Swedish chocolate revolution started in 1992 when Stefan Johnsson Petersén began making chocolates at NK's bakery in Stockholm, where they hadn't made chocolates since World War II. It was an immediate success and NK now makes over 10 tons of chocolate candies for Christmas alone every year. Valhrona chocolate came to our shores that same year. Rose-Marie and Henning Simonsson started Chokladkompaniet in Gothenburg. Kerstin Hallert wrote articles about chocolate in the Swedish press, raising awareness of quality chocolate. We began to make our own chocolates at Vetekatten in Stockholm two years later, with Magnus Johansson and Johan Sörberg in charge. Östen and Agneta Brolin decided to use only Valhrona chocolate in their own chocolates and today large amounts of chocolates are made at Vetekatten. Chocolate tasting is now common throughout the country and the combination of chocolate and wine arouses great interest. I am delighted that many other chocolate-makers have started up in Sweden, some of whom I have helped on their way. An Academy of Chocolate was recently founded, to preserve our traditions and to ensure quality as we continue into the new millennium.

I hope my book can contribute to the delight in, and use of, chocolate. Make sure to follow the recipes carefully, however. Always use scales when weighing—don't take chances with a measuring-jug—then you can't go wrong. Finally I would like to dedicate this book to my dear mother who has always tirelessly listened to my chocolate chatter!

Jan Hedh

Malmö, June 2002

CHAPTER 1

from cacao to chocolate

A short history of chocolate

Legend has it that the god Quetzalcóatl brought cocoa with him. He was the Toltec peoples' god in the north of present-day Mexico. Quetzalcóatl resembled a feathered snake and roamed a paradise where the people worshipped the cacao tree, Cachuaquahitl, from whose fruit the drink of the gods was made.

Quetzalcóatl advised the people on how to cultivate the land and about medicine. He was later betrayed by a priest, Tezcatlipoca, who wanted to govern the country himself. Ever since the disappearance of their god, the Maya, Toltec, and Aztec peoples have awaited his return in another guise. The Aztecs believed that Quetzalcóatl would return in 1519.

The cacao tree has long been cultivated. It is thought that the Maya people have been growing it since 600 AD. Both the Mayas and the Aztecs made beverages from cacao beans. Xocolatl was a drink consisting of husked beans ground in a mortar to an oily, gritty paste. It was flavored with spices such as vanilla and chili, with maize meal being added to fill it out. This cocoa paste was formed into small cakes that were then dried. These cakes were broken and whisked in hot water to make xocolatl.

Montezuma, the Aztec ruler, had a great treasure-trove of stored cocoa beans. According to legend, he drank 50 cups of chocolate a day served in cups of pure gold.

To Europe

Christopher Columbus was the first European to see and feel a cocoa bean, on the island of Guanaja off the coast of Honduras. Columbus took some of these beans back to Spain. The court did not appreciate the cocoa made from these beans, however, so king Ferdinand and queen Isabella missed out on a lucrative source of revenue.

In 1519, the Spanish conquistador Hernán Cortés came into contact with drinking chocolate, large amounts of it being drunk at the court of Montezuma. Some of Cortés' men relayed back information about this chocolate drink, thus making it known in Europe.

Honey was added in order to make this bitter drink more palatable. In Spain, they added sugar cane instead of honey and even began to grow sugar cane for this purpose.

In 1524, Cortés sent a cargo of cocoa beans to Charles V who finally began to appreciate the advantages of cocoa. Being a trader, Cortés was quick to appreciate how money could be made out of cocoa. The Spanish established a monopoly on the import of cocoa, which they retained for 80 years. They saw chocolate as a Spanish specialty and immediately began to grow cocoa in Central America, the Caribbean, Trinidad, Mexico, Haiti, Grenada and Java.

A mixture of sugar cane and vanilla produced an enjoyable drinking chocolate. Having a monopoly, hot chocolate was initially a Spanish specialty. Gradually others came to appreciate the worth of the cocoa bean—first the Dutch, and later Italians, Germans, English, French and Swiss.

Chocolate was introduced to France in 1615 when Anna of Austria, Philip III of Spain's daughter, was married to Louis XIII of France. A letter of 1659, signed by Louis XIV, gave officer David Chaillou the exclusive privilege to sell chocolate, a privilege he retained for 29 years. He opened a shop on the Rue de l'Arbre in Paris. The fashion for eating chocolate began to spread from the court to fashionable society, but it was still relatively unknown among ordinary people.

The use of chocolate as a breakfast drink spread gradually throughout European high society during the 1600s. Chocolate shops were opened where chocolate could be imbibed. Chocolate was rumored to give success with the ladies and to raise potency, which is presumably the reason why the great lover, Giovanni Giacomo Casanova, drank up to 50 cups a day!

Chocolate was also claimed to have medicinal properties. Nevertheless, the development and flavoring of drinking chocolate remained slow and conservative.

Some important dates

1687 Development of the cocoa press.

1756 First mechanized production in France.

1760 Opening of Chocolaterie Royale in Paris. The beans came from French colonies and vanilla for flavoring from Tahiti.

1828 Conrad von Houten made the first cocoa powder.

1875 Henri Nestlé invented dried milk and Tobler made the first milk chocolate. Lindt invented conching.

The cacao tree

The cacao tree, *Theobroma cacao*, belongs to the cacao plant family, *Sterculia ceae*, and originates from the rainy forest area around the Orinoco and Amazon rivers. The tree prefers a temperature of at least 75°F with heavy, evenly distributed rainfall. When cultivated, the cacao plants are first nurtured in small baskets and planted out after 18 months. A cacao tree starts to bear fruit during the fifth year and is at its most productive at ten years.

The cocoa beans used in chocolate factories today come from cacao trees in the so-called cacao belt. This stretches right across America, Asia and Africa between latitudes 20° north and 20° south. The cacao tree grows in a tropical climate together with vanilla, sugar cane and coffee bushes. The tree is often planted beside rivers or on slopes, shaded from sun and wind by banana trees, mango trees and coconut palms.

The soil must be rich in potassium, magnesium and nitrogen. Irrigation is necessary if rainfall is insufficient.

A three-year-old tree is between 10 and 17 feet high, reaching about 27 feet at ten years. The bark, which thickens with age, has a beautiful dark brown color. A cultivated cacao tree has a life of about 30 years, while a wild tree can live up to 50 years. Its roots reach deep and wide round the tree.

The ideal altitude for cultivating cacao is between 1,200 and 1,800 feet above sea level. The tree begins to flower at three years, blooming twice a year thereafter. The beautiful red and white flowers have neither scent nor taste. Only one in a thousand flowers bears fruit. Depending on the type of tree, it takes four to eight months before the flower becomes a pod-like fruit, which grows directly on the trunk.

The ellipse-shaped pod grows to about 8 inches and is firstly orange before maturing to a yellow, copper and orange or russet color.

The pod has a 1 inch leathery outer shell inside which is a sweet, jelly-like pulp containing about 50–60 cacao beans. When the pods have ripened they are cut down. A cacao tree will normally yield about 50 pods a year, giving about four kilos of beans.

Cocoa beans

Three different varieties of cacao trees are grown commercially.
- Criollo is the finest, accounting for about 10 percent of world production.
- Forastero, grown in Amazonia, is of medium quality and accounts for 70 percent of world production.
- Trinitario is of excellent quality and makes up the remaining 20 percent.

Criollo is cultivated in Mexico, Nicaragua, Venezuela, Columbia, on Madagascar and the Comoros islands. The beans are round, pale and well filled. Before fermentation they vary from white to purple, turning light brown after fermentation. Fermentation is easy, the aroma pleasant and the taste mild. Criollo chocolate, such as Valrhona's Grand Cru Manjari, has a reddish hue. The taste of chocolate made from criollo beans is quite fantastic. In my opinion, manjari is the finest and best-tasting chocolate in the world.

Forastero, originating from Amazonia, is the commonest cocoa bean. It grows in Ghana, Nigeria, Ivory Coast, Brazil, Costa Rica, the Dominican Republic, Columbia, Venezuela and Ecuador. The beans are flat and compact. During fermentation, a sour smell and a weak aroma are given off. It has a very bitter taste, and chocolate made from forastero beans alone is extremely dark and bitter.

The trinitario bean is a hybrid of the forastero and criollo beans. It came into being after a cyclone destroyed Trinidad's criollo plantations in 1727. Trinitario gives a better harvest and is more resistant to disease than criollo. It has a finer aroma than forastero, and grows mostly in the same countries as the criollo bean.

Harvest

Harvest takes place all year round, most intensively during November–January and May–July. The pods cannot be picked mechanically and cannot be torn off since this would prevent the re-growth of flowers. The pods are cut off with a machete, making harvesting a very labor-intensive process.

Fermentation

The cocoa bean develops its aroma during fermentation. The fruit pulp containing the cacao beans is poured into a fermenting tub or placed between banana leaves. Fermentation begins at 100–120°F.

Sugar is converted into alcohol during fermentation and a form of lactic acid fermentation begins. During this process, the pulp is broken down and

the bittersweet taste disappears. The beans also develop their brown color. Fermentation is important and must be carefully controlled.

Drying

After drying, the beans contain about 60 percent water. Drying is a difficult process since humidity is often 85–95 percent in the harvesting regions. Beans are spread out on huge mats in a 4 inch thick layer and left to dry in the strong sun for about 14 days. Wood fires or hot air is used in many countries, which are efficient methods but they affect the aroma of the beans.

When the beans have been dried, the remaining fruit pulp and husks are removed. The beans are packed into sacks and sent to central collection points for further transport to coastal harbors.

Processing and raw materials

Roasting

Cocoa beans are roasted at temperatures between 175 and 300°F. Roasting is one of the most important processes in the production of chocolate. Humidity is lowered, flavors released and the shells removed.

Crushing and cleaning

The beans are crushed and cleaned, either before or after roasting, in special cleansing works where the beans' sprouts are separated and sucked off, together with the fragile skins. The less skin remaining the better quality, but it is impossible to avoid some small particles of skin remaining on the kernels.

Milling

Roasting makes the beans fragile and easy to grind in special cocoa mills or rollers. Beans that contain a lot of fat, 50–55 percent, produce heat during the milling process. The rollers convert the beans into a thick, oily cocoa paste. This paste is then either stored in containers or pumped directly to the presses or mixers. Cocoa paste is the raw material for cocoa powder production.

Cocoa powder

High quality cocoa powder has to meet stringent standards for flavor and solubility. The kinds of beans used for cocoa paste have to be chosen with the utmost care. Cocoa powder should not contain more than 20–25 percent cocoa fat. Half of the fat (cocoa butter) is pressed out of the paste in large hydraulic presses at a pressure of 450 lb/in². The compressed "cake" that now remains is 2 inches thick and consists of pure cocoa and the remaining fat.

The "cake" is taken out, cooled, crushed, finely milled and sifted several times. The taste, fat percentage, and granule size are controlled in the laboratory before the powder is ready for packaging.

Depending on the pressure used, two kinds of cocoa powder are produced:

- cocoa powder with a low fat percentage, 10–12 percent cocoa butter.
- cocoa powder with 20–22 percent cocoa butter.

Cocoa butter

The rest of the "cake" consists of cocoa butter. Untreated cocoa butter has the same acrid taste and smell as non-roasted cocoa beans. A special process is required to improve the taste of the butter. It is filtered very carefully and the fat, which has been heated to a high temperature (300–400°F), is steamed in a powerful vacuum. The steam removes the unwanted flavors.

Cocoa butter gives the chocolate a suitable melting point so that it can withstand normal temperatures and yet melt pleasantly in the mouth. Cocoa butter also gives the chocolate a hard, brittle consistency, a nice luster, a beautiful appearance and a long shelf life.

Other raw materials in chocolate

Sugar

Sugar is a product from sugar beet or sugar cane. Beet and sugar cane are chemically identical products. Sugar cane has a distinct taste if not properly refined.

Powdered milk

Powdered milk is a very important ingredient, particularly in milk chocolate and white chocolate. Depending on the type of chocolate, the following kinds of powdered milk are used:
- low-fat
- spray-dried with a high fat-content
- roller-dried with a high fat-content
- creamy milk crumbs

Milk crumbs are produced in a special drying process. Condensed milk is dried and sugar added, to give an extremely smooth and creamy caramel flavor.

Soy lecithin

Soy lecithin is a natural oil-like product. The dosage of lecithin varies between 0 and 0.5 percent. Soy lecithin is the only permitted emulsifier in the world. An emulsifier forms a "bridge" between water and oil. Soy lecithin makes it possible for the cocoa butter to bind together the sugar, powdered milk and the dry materials of the cocoa "cake."

Vanilla and vanillin

Vanillin is most commonly used in flavoring. Vanillin has a similar aroma to vanilla but is chemically produced. Valrhona's chocolate factory, however, uses only real vanilla.

Good to know

Cocoa butter has a melting point of 95°F, which means that chocolates made with cocoa butter melt beautifully in the mouth.

Chocolate production

Having looked at raw materials, we can now turn to the production process itself.

Mixing

Firstly, the ingredients are mixed together:
Bittersweet or semisweet chocolate
- sugar
- cocoa paste
- cocoa butter

For milk chocolate, powdered milk is added

White chocolate
- sugar
- cocoa butter
- powdered milk

Any additional additives are mixed in at this stage. The resultant mixture is chocolate "dough."

Fine rolling

After intensive mixing, the dough-like product is run between rollers. This refining process ensures that no grains can be detected on the tongue, and changes the dough into a fine powder.

Conching—heat treatment

The finely rolled powder is conched for several hours. Conching is an intensive technical treatment that produces heat. Heat has the following effects, for example:
- the moisture in the powder swells
- the acrid flavors disappear
- pleasant flavors are developed by the contact between sugar, powdered milk and cocoa butter
- the cocoa butter dissolves slowly, giving the chocolate a certain kind of liquidity

Conching is the third important process in the development of flavor. It is such an important process that it is divided into two processes or steps:

- dry conching—to produce the optimal distribution of flavorings and a certain amount of liquidity.
- liquid conching—where the remaining cocoa butter is added to give the correct fat-content for the kind of chocolate under production.

Solid or liquid

The liquid chocolate is now ready for tempering and molding into blocks or making chips.

Valrhona's Grand Cru types, Guanaja, Manjari, and Pur Caraïbe are conched for five days.

Tempering

Finally, the chocolate mass is tempered to give the desired qualities. About one third of chocolate consists of fat from the cocoa mass, cocoa paste and powdered milk. Only the fat is affected by tempering. The chocolate is cooled and crystallized so that it will harden in the correct way after molding.

Reasons for tempering chocolate
Correct tempering and treatment of the cocoa butter gives the resultant chocolate the following qualities:

- appealing luster
- beautiful color
- correct brittleness or "snap"
- soft, melting consistency
- ability to shrink and loosen from the molds

Incorrect tempering leads to the following problems:

- peckled chocolate
- grainy, short structure
- quick melting on contact
- does not shrink, and fastens in the molds

Three factors are always important:

Time-movement-temperature

These three factors are of the utmost importance. If any of them is missing it will be impossible to temper the chocolate. The purpose of tempering is to create as small crystals as possible. The luster of the chocolate depends entirely on the position of these crystals—the flatter they lay in proximity to each other, the finer the luster.

There are three kinds of fat crystals in cocoa butter: alpha, beta and gamma. Only the beta form is stable. The others are instable and have a lower melting point and a tendency to form stable crystals after a while, which leads to the formation of grey specks. Tempering controls the process so that only stable beta crystals remain in the chocolate.

Five types of crystals are formed in all during tempering: besides the alpha and gamma crystals, the beta crystal divides into beta, beta 2 and primary crystals.

CHAPTER 2

Valrhona Chocolate

A whole new world of chocolate was opened for me when I first came into contact with Valrhona's chocolate from France. In 1993, Rose-Marie and Henning Simonsson secured the agency for Valrhona in Sweden. The following year we held courses in chocolate handling in Gothenburg, Stockholm and Eslöv. We also taught the finest restaurants in Sweden how to work with real chocolate, particularly in desserts and truffles.

Valrhona's chocolate factory lies at the heart of the Rhône valley in Tain l'Hermitage, a typical sleepy southern French town. The factory stands in the main street with its store and school at the back. Their school of chocolate is headed by Frédric Bau and is highly recommended.

Valrhona were the first to manufacture chocolate using the same criteria as winemakers, so-called Grand Cru, with extra high demands and specifications as to the type and quality of beans used. Subsequently, the world's first vintage chocolate was produced—Gran Couva 68% from Trinidad, which contains trinitario beans from one plantation alone ("Single Estate Chocolate"). The result was a great success and the first harvest in 1999 from Gran Couva and the San Juan Estate on Trinidad was of exceptionally high quality.

This was the first time that chocolate had been made with beans from just one plantation. Beans are usually mixed from different regions to achieve the optimal flavor. The extremely high quality of the San Juan beans allowed for the production of "Single Estate Chocolate."

The Montserra plateau has dark, so-called chocolate soil (terre de chocolat). Gran Couva chocolate has a reddish-brown color, an intense full flavor and a long aftertaste.

Valrhona has used high-aroma trinitario beans from different plantations on Trinidad for their Grand Cru Pur Caraïbe. Using the 1999 harvest, the 2000 vintage came from Chuao Valley in Venezuela, containing 64 percent cocoa beans of fantastic quality, pleasant tartness and with a scent of raspberry.

Valrhona is considered to be the foremost producer of high quality chocolate. Their three finest varieties are named "Les Grands Crus de Chocolat." Many call Valrhona the Rolls Royce of chocolate and I can only agree. I have never tasted anything like it!

Valrhona's types of chocolate

Guanaja
70% Grand Cru

45% trinitario, 45% criollo and 10% forastero beans from the island of Guanaja. Perhaps the most intense chocolate in the world. Long aftertaste and fine balance.

Manjari
64% Grand Cru

100% criollo beans from different countries in the Indian Ocean. Fruity taste of raspberry and vanilla.

Pur Caraïbe
66% Grand Cru

100% trinitario beans from the Caribbean, Trinidad in particular. Exquisitely balanced taste with rounded tones of mature berries and vanilla.

Valrhona Caraque 56%
The cocoa percentage gives it a perfect consistency for coating candy and making gourmet chocolates. The mixture of criollo and forastero beans gives a fine, mature chocolate flavor.

Jivara Lactée
40% Grand Cru

Milk chocolate with an aroma of vanilla and caramel. Unusually high cocoa content.

Ivoire
White chocolate

Contains relatively little sugar, has a melting consistency and is perfumed with the best vanilla.

Cacao Pâte Extra 100
Pure cocoa paste with no sugar added. Powerful, condensed taste. Used to heighten chocolate flavor, and in baking. Free from lecithin.

For milk chocolate, I recommend Valrhona Jivara Lactée with 40 percent cocoa. Such a high percentage is unusual for milk chocolate. This chocolate has a mature flavor of fresh milk, sugar and cocoa butter with undertones of vanilla and caramel.

For white chocolate for use in coating I recommend Valrhona Ivoire, which consists of cocoa butter, milk, vanilla and sugar. A very fine melting consistency, with lower sugar content than usual for white chocolate.

I specify Marabou (a Swedish brand) chocolate as a substitute for Valrhona in my recipes. You can, of course, use other chocolate brands with more or less the same cocoa content. When I specify a particular chocolate it is based on my experience of working with just that type. The type of chocolate varies the flavor and its cocoa content influences the consistency of your cakes, cookies and candies.

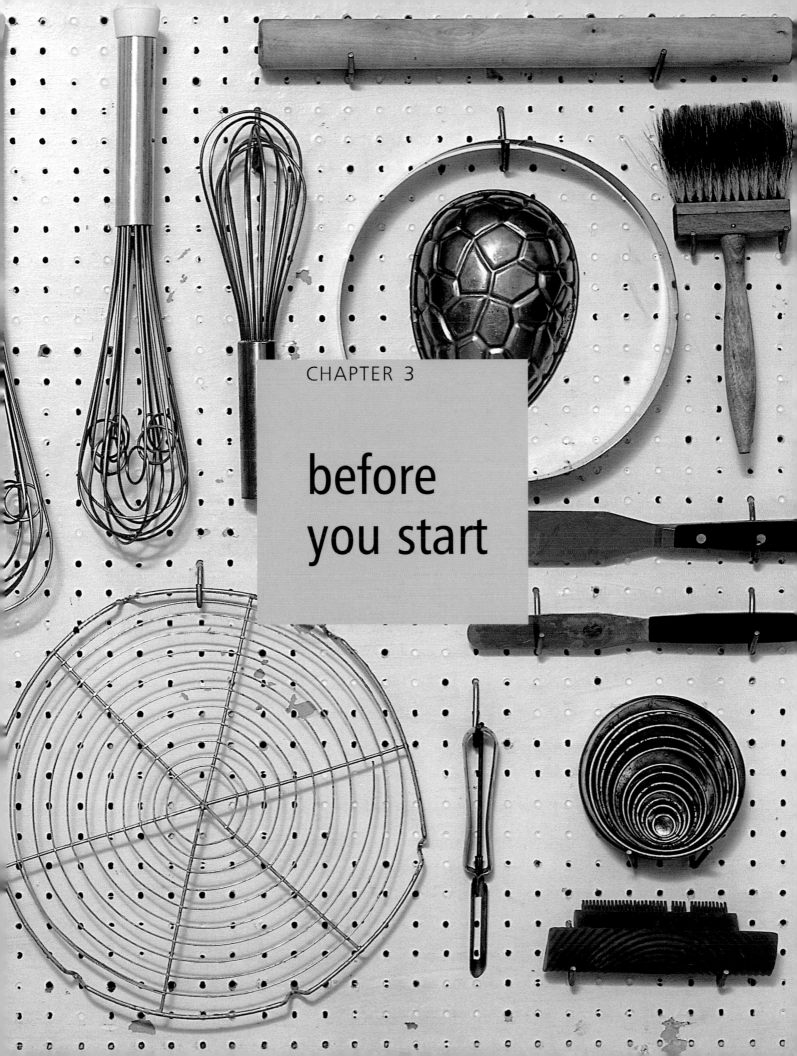

CHAPTER 3

before
you start

Chocolate techniques

It is important to use high-quality ingredients as far as possible.

1. Always use dairy butter, not margarine. I recommend unsalted butter, since this is fresher than salted.
2. Always use real cream and not synthetic cream.
3. Always buy good, quality chocolate, preferably Valrhona. This has the best quality and a high cocoa content. It costs a little more than other chocolate but tastes infinitely better. Read more about Valrhona on p. 30.
4. Never use synthetic vanilla but always vanilla pods, preferably vanilla from Tahiti, which has a nicely rounded aromatic taste.
5. Try to get hold of almonds from the Mediterranean, preferably Italy or Spain. These have so much more taste than almonds from California.
6. Use ordinary, all-purpose flour in the recipes unless otherwise specified. Wheat flour contains more gluten and is not suitable for this kind of baking.

Some useful tips

Take time to plan. Nothing feels too onerous if you are methodical and plan in advance. Sometimes you have to start the day before to allow flavors to mature and produce the tastiest result. Occasionally, you may need to start a whole week or more in advance.

When I'm using baking sheets I usually use a so-called baking cloth. This is a silicon-prepared cloth that can be bought in most supermarkets. If you want to be really professional, buy one or two silpat cloths for baking on. These last for years and nothing sticks to the surface.

Unused egg whites can be frozen. If you have leftover egg yolks, add 10% sugar and stir until the sugar has melted before putting them in the freezer. If you freeze the yolks without sugar they become grainy and cannot be used.

Remember to serve cakes and desserts at their right temperatures for optimal taste and consistency. Frozen desserts can be thawed in the refrigerator until they achieve the right consistency. This usually takes about half an hour. Cold chocolate desserts are usually served too cold, 40–50°F is optimal. Cakes should be served at 50–55°F and soufflés should be served at 40–50°F.

Weights and volumes

In order to achieve a really successful result, the ingredients have to have the correct relative proportions. Get in the habit of always weighing the ingredients, which are mostly given in weight rather than volume in the recipes. Correct amounts are by far the most important component for achieving good results in this kind of baking and dessert making. Always use good scales, preferably digital.

Even liquid ingredients such as cream and water are almost always given in ounces with cups or fl. oz. in brackets, because even small variations can make a big difference. Where tablespoon (tbs) or teaspoon (tsp) occur, this refers to the standard measures found in the stores.

Grade of difficulty

●

Not at all difficult if you plan ahead.

● ●

A degree of proficiency required and quite a lot of time. For a rainy day.

● ● ●

You've decided to do something quite fantastic and to spend a lot of time and care on your creation!

Tempering—working with chocolate

To be able to work, "mold," or dip chocolate, you have to learn how to temper the chocolate, or rather the cocoa butter in the chocolate. It is only the cocoa butter that is changed by tempering. If you do not temper the chocolate before starting, it will become gray and dull. It will not shrink, and will therefore fasten in the molds.

Objects to be dipped in chocolate should be kept at 70°F, to give a beautiful shiny surface. Never dip anything cold into tempered chocolate, for this will turn the chocolate gray and dull, hardening from the inside rather than the outside.

Different types of chocolate are tempered at different temperatures. White chocolate and milk chocolate have a lower melting point, so tempering is done at a lower temperature.

Equipment

Precise control of temperatures is crucial during tempering. It is best to use a thermometer graded up to 125°F. (An ordinary digital oven thermometer will do.) You also need a small marble slab and preferably a microwave oven, spatula and a plastic bowl for melting chocolate in. When tempering milk chocolate or white chocolate do not exceed 115°F. These two kinds of chocolate contain the protein casein, which "bunches" at 130°F, completely ruining the chocolate.

Never melt directly on the stove
Melt very carefully in a microwave oven so that the chocolate does not burn. Stir often and do not use metal objects. You can also use a double boiler or a bowl placed in a saucepan of simmering water. Avoid moisture from the steam and stir often, since the water can be 180–190°F.

So-called fat bloom, gray chocolate. The fat has floated up to the surface and the chocolate has turned gray because of incorrect tempering.

The chocolate is tabled...

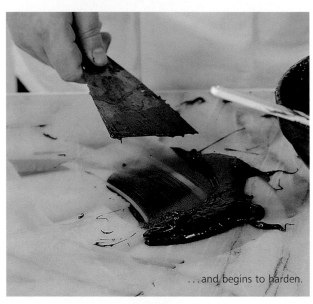
...and begins to harden.

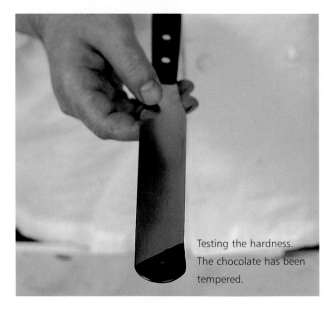
Testing the hardness.
The chocolate has been
tempered.

Method 1—seeding
1. Firstly chop the chocolate.
2. Warm half the amount to 117–122°F for dark chocolate, 113°F for milk chocolate and 105°F for white chocolate. Then stir in the remaining chocolate.
3. Stir until the temperature reaches 80–82°F for dark chocolate, 79–81°F for milk chocolate and 77–79°F for white chocolate. Then heat to 88–90°F for dark chocolate, 84–86°F for milk chocolate and 82–84°F for white chocolate. It is easiest to do this in a microwave oven.

Method 2—tabling (commonest among professionals)
1. Heat the chocolate to the correct temperature.
2. Pour out 3/4 of the chocolate onto a marble slab. Smooth backwards and forwards until the chocolate begins to harden.
3. Scrape off the chocolate and mix it back into the remaining 1/4.
4. Heat to the right temperature, stirring all the time.

Bittersweet or semisweet chocolate:
Heat to 115–122°F. Cool to 80–82°F and then heat to 88–90°F.
Milk chocolate:
Heat to 113°F. Cool to 79–81°F and then heat to 86°F.
White chocolate:
Heat to 104°F. Cool to 77–79°F and then heat to 82–84°F.

Molding chocolate shells or figures
Use plastic or metal molds. These can be bought at a hobby store. More professional molds can be found at specialized kitchen stores. You can even use toy molds intended for the sandpit! Polish the mold or molds with some cotton wool before using.

Fill the mold, which should be able to withstand 70°F, with tempered chocolate. If you want to use more than one kind of tempered chocolate: firstly splash the mold with the one kind and then pour in the other kind. Knock the molds on the table to remove air bubbles from the chocolate. After about one minute, turn the mold upside down on a rack and let excess chocolate run off. Just before the chocolate hardens, scrape the

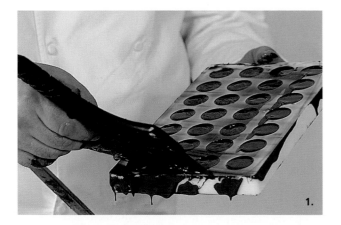

surface with a spatula or pastry scraper. Put the mold into the refrigerator and leave for 30 minutes for the chocolate to shrink and loosen from the mold. If the chocolate does not loosen from the mold, return to the refrigerator until ready.

Molding chocolate in cocoa powder

1. Sift the cocoa powder into a suitable container and smooth with a ruler. Carefully press the object you wish to reproduce in the powder to make a mold.
2. Carefully fill the mold with tempered chocolate and leave to cool for 60 minutes.
3. Lift out the figure and brush off excess powder.

Gelatin molds

Using gelatin will give you great scope to mold all sorts of exciting objects. Making your own molds is part of the confectioner's trade.

Put a suitable object, which you wish to make a mold from, in a plastic container and pour hot gelatin mixture over it. Leave to solidify. Remove the object and clean the resulting gelatin mold with a knife.

Temper the chocolate and fill the gelatin mold, knocking it on the table several times to remove air pockets. Place in the refrigerator to solidify, about 30 minutes according to size.

Carefully remove the molded object from the gelatin mold (using washing-up gloves to avoid thumbprints on the chocolate).

8.8 oz (250 g) gelatin sheets
13 oz (375 g) water
11 oz (315 g) sugar
2.6 oz (75 g) glucose

1. Immerse the gelatin sheets in plenty of cold water for about 10 minutes.
2. Pour water, sugar and glucose into a saucepan. Bring to a boil and skim the sugar syrup.
3. Drain the gelatin sheets in a colander and mix them into the hot sugar syrup until they melt.
4. If you wish to use the gelatin mold many times, store in the freezer and it will keep its shape and not shrink.

1. Excess chocolate is scraped off after the mold has been knocked on the table.
2. The chilled chocolate shells have been removed from their molds.
3. Molding in cocoa powder.
4. Molding in a gelatin mold.

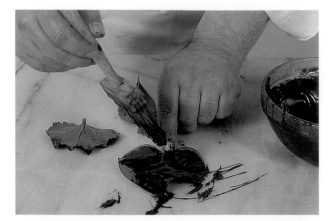

Chocolate leaves
Use freshly picked leaves that have pronounced veins. Temper bittersweet or semisweet chocolate. Brush a thin layer of chocolate on the underside of the leaf. Leave to cool. Brush again. Place in the refrigerator for 10 minutes to harden (crystallize). Carefully remove the fresh leaf from the chocolate. The leaf can be kept for decoration.

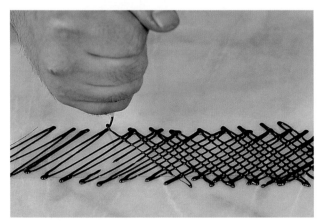

Chocolate latticework
Temper bittersweet or semisweet chocolate; see p. 35. Cut an ordinary plastic case (not acetate film) into 1/4 inch strips. Pipe a latticework frame. Form into a roll, with the joint downwards. When the roll has hardened, place in the refrigerator for 10 minutes to crystallize.

Take out the roll and carefully remove the plastic. Use a hot knife to divide the roll into shorter sections if required.

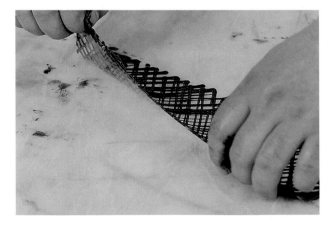

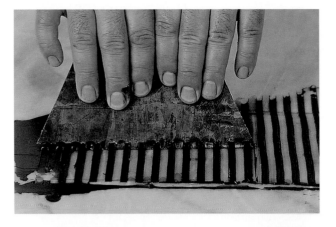

Chocolate loops

Temper dark chocolate; see p. 35. Spread out a thin layer on acetate film. Make strips by pulling a glue scraper towards you. Wait until the chocolate begins to harden (crystallize). Fold the film over and press the ends gently together to form a row of loops. Leave the chocolate in the refrigerator for 5 minutes. Remove the acetate film.

Chocolate is scraped with a glue scraper.

Fold over the plastic film and press the open ends together.

Loosen the plastic after cooling.

Piped chocolate decoration

Temper the chocolate; see p. 35. Pour it into a paper cone. Pipe decorations and leave the chocolate to harden (crystallize).

Fans (without tempering)

Heat the chocolate to 113°F. Spread the chocolate thinly on a marble slab. Spread the chocolate until it has a special sound. Place your finger as shown in the picture. Push the pallet knife forward quickly, with your finger on top. Make sure the chocolate curls over your index finger. Practice a few times. Re-melt the chocolate occasionally.

Professional method: Heat a baking sheet to 113°F. Spread out 113°F chocolate really thinly. Put the sheet in the refrigerator and let the chocolate harden (crystallize). Then remove and bring to room temperature. Make the fan according to the description above and according to the photos.

Fans, chocolate spaghetti, cigarettes, etc., *are made with un-tempered chocolate.*

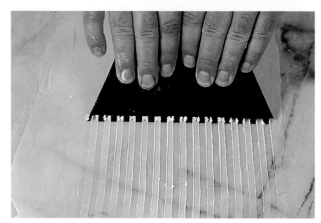

Chocolate cigarettes (without tempering)

Heat the chocolate to 113°F. Spread the chocolate thinly on a marble slab until it makes a special sound. Push the scraper forwards, pressing out "cigarettes."

I have previously spread out a thin layer of white chocolate and made stripes with a glue scraper, then allowed the chocolate to harden (crystallize).

After this, I have spread the thin layer of bittersweet chocolate on top. It is best to practice using one kind of chocolate.

Chocolate shavings (without tempering)

Heat 7 oz (200 g) chocolate to 113°F. Spread the chocolate, preferably on a marble slab, otherwise use a draining board or other cold work surface. Spread backwards and forwards with a spatula or pallet knife until the chocolate begins to harden. Make large shavings using a scraper. This can be done with both white and dark chocolate.

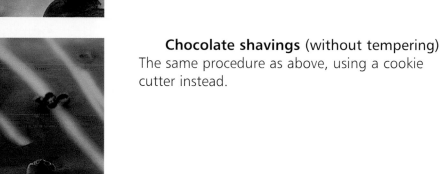

Chocolate shavings (without tempering)

The same procedure as above, using a cookie cutter instead.

Chocolate spaghetti (without tempering)

This method can be used in many different ways. You can make threads, birds nests and spaghetti, for example. Heat 7 oz (200 g) dark chocolate to 113°F (no tempering). Leave a metal tray in the freezer for 10 minutes. Make a paper cone with a very small hole in it. Fill the cone and pipe parallel threads onto the cold tray. Immediately, before the threads are too hard, remove them with a spatula or pallet knife. Shape the threads as required. Leave them for about an hour in the refrigerator until the chocolate has hardened (crystallized). Store in a cool place.

Above: The chocolate is piped on to the tray.

The threads are loosened with a spatula from the frozen tray.

Marbling chocolate

Spread a thin layer of tempered chocolate onto plastic film.

Make patterns with a glue scraper or wood grainer. Leave to harden.

Spread a thin layer of chocolate on top.

Pour out different kinds of tempered chocolate and spread them backwards and forwards to produce a marbled effect. You can also spread the chocolate on bubble wrap.

Put the plastic on a tray and let the chocolate harden (crystallize) for about 10 minutes. Put a tray on top of the chocolate to prevent it curling at the edges. Loosen from the plastic and break off pieces for decoration.

If you want to make squares, cut them out before the chocolate has completely hardened.

Chocolate marbling

You can marble chocolate in many different ways. Pictures 1–3 show one example. You can also use a glue scraper, brush or sponge.

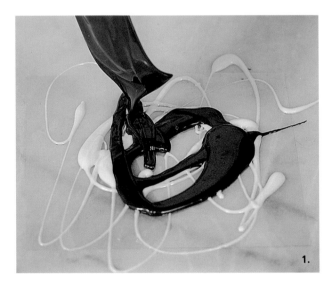

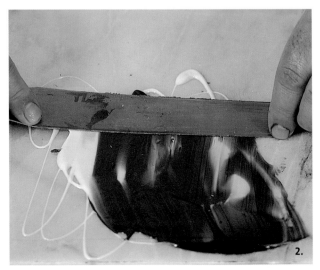

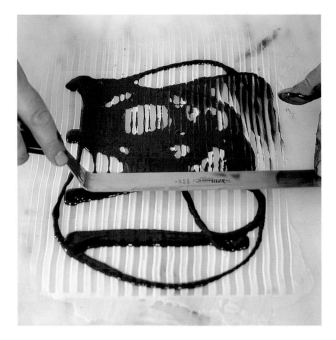 

Chocolate roses

0.5 oz (15 g) sugar
2 tsp (10 g) water
7 oz (200 g) semisweet chocolate (Valrhona Caraque
    56% or Marabou dark)
2 oz (60 g) glucose or honey (non-liquid)

1. Mix sugar and water in a saucepan, bring to a boil and leave to cool.
2. Melt the chocolate in a microwave oven, stirring occasionally. Bring to 130°F.
3. Mix the chocolate with the sugar syrup and glucose or honey. Using a spoon, mix to a paste.
4. Leave to stiffen for 1 hour in a plastic bag.
5. Knead into a pliable paste and make rose petals with a spatula. Form the petals into a rose shape.
6. Single petals can be used for decoration.

Tip
This is also known as Spanish modeling chocolate and can be shaped in the same way as marzipan. If you wish to use milk or white chocolate, reduce the glucose to 1.4 oz (40 g) since these kinds of chocolate are softer.

Boiling sugar

Sugar is boiled to produce more or less concentrated sugar syrup. Glucose is added to make the sugar light and easy to work with.

As soon as the sugar has reached the required temperature, remove the saucepan from the heat. Put the saucepan in a bowl of cold water for a few moments to prevent further boiling.

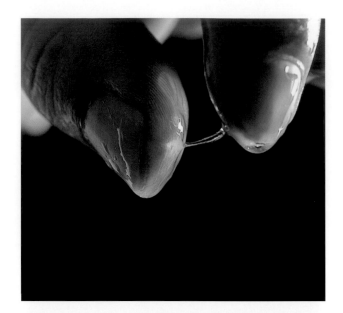

Equipment for boiling sugar
A sugar thermometer is preferable since temperatures must be measured carefully. Otherwise you can use cold water and do a so-called finger test.

A brush is needed to keep the sides of the saucepan free from sugar crystals during boiling.

Preferably use an unlined copper saucepan, which is a good heat-inducer and prevents burning. An ordinary stainless steel saucepan can also be used.

A thermometer graded up to 355°F is a highly recommendable investment.

Measuring sugar temperatures
If you don't have a sugar thermometer you can, however, do a manual test.

Dip your thumb and index finger in a bowl of cold water. Then quickly pick up a small amount of caramel with your fingers and dip them quickly back into the water. A thread or ball test can be made in this way. You can also use a spoon instead if you don't want to risk getting burned.

Above, thread test, and below, the hard ball test.

Sugar temperature
The most usual temperatures for boiling sugar are:
  Thread test 234–242°F
  Ball test 244–248°F
  Fondant 244°F
  Marzipan 252°F
  Hard ball test 252–264°F
  Toffee test 244°F
  Weak caramel test 295–313°F
Caramelizing
  Strong caramel test 313–336°F
  Drawn or blown caramel

Fondant
Fondant means melting. By using so-called tabling (smoothing the paste backwards and forwards until it begins to harden) the sugar crystals become smaller making the glaze smooth and pliable. This kind of glaze does not dry out and lose its luster as a so-called water glaze, made of confectioners' sugar and water, would.

Storage
Can be kept in the refrigerator for several weeks.

Butter is used to separate the caramelized almonds.

Caramelizing almonds and nuts

Caramelized almonds and nut kernels are a real finesse, for use in mousse and ice cream or for dipping in chocolate.

The addition of lemon juice makes the sugar soluble and speeds caramelizing. A little dab of butter adds flavor and keeps the nuts separate. If the temperature is too low, the caramel surface will be too chewy. Put the almonds back in the saucepan and re-heat.

3.5 oz (100 g) almonds, hazelnut, walnut or pistachio
    kernels
0.5 oz (4 tsp) sugar
0.2 oz (2 tsp) pressed lemon juice
0.2 oz (1 tsp) butter

1. Melt the sugar and lemon juice until golden. Pour in the almonds/nut kernels. Stir until covered with caramel.
2. Stir in the butter and pour out onto a baking cloth, preferably silpat. Separate the nuts after a few minutes. Leave to cool.

Ladle and spoon test

Rose test

Dip the ladle in the sauce. Lift out and blow on the underside. If the sauce "wrinkles" and forms a rose-like pattern it is ready.

Spoon test

Lift out the spoon and run your finger through the sauce. If the sauce does not re-form it is ready.

Chocolate glaze

Dip the spoon into the glaze. It should drip, not run.

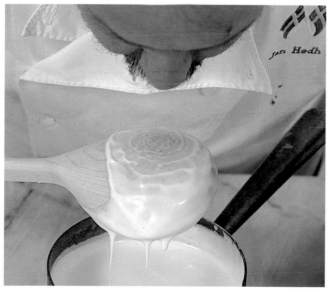

Is the sauce ready? The rose test will provide the answer.

CHAPTER 4

chocolate
candies

In Sweden, we use the word "praline" for all kinds of chocolate confections. This name originated from the Marquise de Praliné who caramelized almonds to make candy. Pralines, or chocolate candies with exciting fillings, rank amongst the most prestigious creations of a good pastry chef. High quality chocolate confectionary has always been the jewel in the crown of a top-class patisserie.

It was during my education in Switzerland that I first began to understand what chocolate really was. We usually used Lindt or Suchard chocolate. Switzerland, like France and Belgium, has always been an outstanding chocolate country, with artisan chocolate-makers to be found in towns both large and small. Swiss chocolate has always been of a very high quality, with melting truffles as their great specialty.

I still remember the special scent of chocolate every morning when I attended the Coba School in Basel, and the tastes of the hundreds of different kinds of chocolates we made there. Julius Perlia, the head and creative leader of the school, also ran a chocolate store, Confiserie Zoo, where the school's confections were sold. During my time there, I used to do extra work at Confiserie Brändli (on Barfusserplatz in the old town), which was number one in those days. The head chocolatier, Beni Schmied, was formidably strict about the quality and appearance of company products.

Later, when I had begun to work at Confiserie Honold in Zurich, I was impressed by their incredible range of high-quality chocolate confections. We usually used Suchard chocolate since our greatest competitors, Confiserie Sprüngli, owned the Lindt & Sprüngli chocolate factory. Sprüngli is one of the largest manufacturers of handmade confectionery, employing several hundred pastry chefs, and selling quite fantastic chocolate candies and cakes in their stores.

Ganache

Many chocolates contain ganache, which is also known as truffle. Ganache is usually made of cream and chocolate and should be quite firm, shiny and pliable. Butter and glucose or honey are added to make the ganache keep better and to give it a melting consistency.

You will need a greater percentage of chocolate in ganache intended for cutting into strips than for ganache used for filling chocolate shells. Ganache used for filling should have a softer consistency.

Dipping candy

1. Always use a thermometer when tempering chocolate.
2. Never dip cold candy in chocolate since this will give rise to fat-bloom (when the cocoa butter floats to the surface of the chocolate, making it dull and moist).
3. The candy should be at room temperature (68°F) so that the resulting chocolate will have a beautiful luster.
4. Ideally there should be a 50°F difference between the chocolate and the candy that is to be dipped.
5. Always use at least 7 oz (200 g) chocolate when you are dipping candy. Any excess chocolate can be kept in plastic wrap for use on another occasion.
6. Tilting the bowl makes dipping easier. Re-heat the chocolate as soon as it begins to solidify.

Storage
Never keep chocolate candy in the refrigerator. The ideal storage temperature is 60–65°F.

Pistachio Ganache makes about 30

• •

You can buy pistachios (preferably from Sicily, which are the greenest and tastiest) ready-shelled. Adding orange-flower water brings out and heightens the pistachio flavor. Orange-flower water can be bought in most herb stores. See photo, p. 65.

Pistachio ganache

1 oz (30 g) pistachios, shelled
6.3 oz (180 g) white chocolate (Valrhona Ivoire, Lindt or Callebaut)
2.8 oz (80 g) heavy cream (1/2 cup)
0.4 oz (10 g) orange-flower honey
1.2 oz (35 g) unsalted butter, room temperature
1/2 tsp (2 g) orange-flower water
confectioners' sugar (for powdering hands when rolling)

For coating

7 oz (200 g) white chocolate (Valrhona Ivoire, Lindt, Callebaut or Fazer)
1.8 oz (50 g) pistachios for decoration

DAY 1

Make the pistachio ganache

1. Grind the pistachios, in a mortar or in a food processor, to a smooth paste.
2. Finely chop the chocolate and pour into a small microwave bowl.
3. Boil the cream and honey and pour over the chopped chocolate.
4. Stir with a plastic spoon, or use a hand blender, to make the ganache smooth and pliable.
5. Insert a thermometer into the ganache. At 95–104°F, stir in the butter, pistachio purée and orange-flower water. Pour the ganache into a bowl and let it stiffen, covered with plastic wrap, ideally at 54–59°F for about 24 hours.

DAY 2

6. Using a plastic pastry bag with a smooth no. 8 tip, fill with ganache and pipe out 0.4 oz (10 g) balls onto parchment paper. Leave for 3 hours in a cool place.
   Sift over confectioner's sugar. Cover your palms with confectioner's sugar and roll the ganache into smooth balls. Leave to firm on the parchment paper for 3 hours.
7. Temper the chocolate; see p. 35. Roll the balls in the tempered chocolate and replace on the parchment paper to harden.
8. Roll the balls in the chocolate a second time and decorate with a pistachio.

Worth knowing

A ganache is an emulsifier and should have a quite firm, but pliable, consistency.

Raspberry Diamonds makes about 24

• • •

Manjari chocolate has an acidity that makes it perfect for raspberries. Criollo beans from the Indian Ocean have a sharp, fruity flavor and a beautiful russet color. My absolute favorite chocolate! See p. 83.

1 multi-cavity candy mold, preferably diamond shapes

Raspberry ganache for the filling

1.8 oz (50 g) bittersweet chocolate (Valrhona Grand Cru Manjari 64.5% or Marabou dark)
3.5 oz (100 g) raspberry purée, about 5.3 oz (150 g) frozen berries
0.9 oz (25 g) unsalted butter, room temperature
0.4 oz (10 g) Eau de Vie au Framboise or Cointreau (2 tsp)
0.7 oz (20 g) honey

For molding

7 oz (200 g) semisweet chocolate (Valrhona Caraque 56% or Marabou dark)
raspberries preserved in Eau de Vie au Framboise; see p. 82.

1. Finely chop the chocolate and place into a microwave-safe bowl.
2. Strain the raspberries through a sieve into a saucepan and boil down to 2.6 oz (75 g). Pour them over the chocolate and mix with a plastic spoon or a hand blender into an even, pliable ganache.
3. Put a thermometer in the ganache. Mix in the butter, liquor and honey at 95–104°F.
4. Melt and temper the semisweet chocolate; see p. 35. Make the chocolate molds and leave to harden in the refrigerator; see molding p. 36.
5. Drain the preserved raspberries in a colander.
6. The ganache should not be more than 81–82°F when used to fill the chocolates. The chocolate in the molds will melt if the ganache is too hot.
7. Using a paper cone, half fill the chocolate molds with ganache.
8. Place half a raspberry in each mold and 3/4 fill with the remaining ganache. Cool at 54–59°F.
9. Heat up and temper the remaining semisweet chocolate. Pour over to cover the filling and smooth off.
10. Place in the refrigerator for 30 minutes to harden. Knock out the candies onto parchment paper. Let the mold return to room temperature and repeat the procedure.

Chestnut Ganache   makes about 30

• • •

This delicious, easy-to-make candy gets its beautiful creaminess from the chestnut cream and its special flavor from the rum. Pure Caraïbe chocolate balances the chestnut cream perfectly. A wonderful autumn treat! See photo, p. 70.

Chestnut ganache

5.3 oz (150 g) bittersweet chocolate (Valrhona Grand Pur Caraïbe 66.5% or Marabou dark)
1.8 oz (50 g) milk chocolate (Valrhona Jivara Lactée 40% or Marabou milk chocolate)
3.5 oz (100 g) heavy cream (1/2 cup)
3.5 oz (100 g) chestnuts, crème de marron, preserved
1.4 oz (40 g) unsalted butter, room temperature
0.9 oz (25 g) dark rum (1/8 cup)

For coating

7 oz (200 g) semisweet chocolate (Valrhona Caraque 56% or Marabou dark)

DAY 1
Make the chestnut ganache

1. Finely chop the chocolate and place in a microwave bowl.
2. Boil the cream in a small saucepan and pour it over the chocolate. Stir with a plastic spoon or hand blender to a smooth, pliable ganache.
3. Add the chestnut cream.
4. Put a thermometer in the ganache. At 95–104°F, mix in the butter and rum. Pour into a container and leave in room temperature for 24 hours.

DAY 2

5. Using a pastry bag with a smooth no. 8 tip, pipe out 0.4 oz (10 g) crests of ganache, as in the photo. Leave to stiffen for about 3 hours.
6. Temper the chocolate; see p. 35. With a fork, dip the crests into the chocolate. Tap the fork on edge of bowl to remove excess chocolate. Leave on parchment paper to harden.

Bitter Chocolate Ganache Grand Cru Guanaja   makes about 25

• •

Guanaja probably has the deepest and most intense taste of all kinds of chocolate.

Ganache

7.7 oz (220 g) bittersweet chocolate (Valrhona Grand Cru Guanaja 70.5% or Marabou dark)
6.7 oz (190 g) heavy cream (3/4 cup)

1.4 oz (40 g) honey
1.4 oz (40 g) unsalted butter, room temperature

For coating

7 oz (200 g) semisweet chocolate (Valrhona Caraque 56% or Marabou dark)
cocoa powder for sifting over

Follow the recipe for Palet D'or Pur Caraïbe, p. 52, but omit the gold leaf and sift over with cocoa powder instead. See photo, p. 53.

Chocolate Truffle   makes about 40

• •

See photo, p. 1.

8.8 oz (250 g) bittersweet chocolate (Valrhona Guanaja 70.5% or Marabou dark)
or 10.5 oz (300 g) milk chocolate (Valrhona Jivara lactée 40%)
or 10.5 oz (300 g) white chocolate (Valrhona Ivoire)
1/2 vanilla pod
3.5 oz (100 g) heavy cream (1/2 cup)
2.8 oz (80 g) neutrally tasting honey
1.8 oz (50 g) unsalted butter
7 oz (200 g) chocolate, of the same sort as chosen above, for dipping
2.8 oz (80 g) cocoa powder (preferably Valrhona)
or confectioners' sugar (for white chocolate)

1. Finely chop the chocolate. Briefly run in a blender or food processor.
2. Open the vanilla pod. Scrape the seeds into a saucepan and add the cream and honey.
3. Boil up the cream mixture and pour it over the chocolate. Mix to an even paste and add the butter.
4. Spread the chocolate on a plate and cover with plastic wrap. Leave to cool at room temperature until firm.
5. Using a pastry bag with a no. 10 tip, pipe out small balls of chocolate, about 1 inch in diameter, onto parchment paper. Leave in the refrigerator to stiffen.
6. Cover your palms with a little cocoa powder and roll the truffle into smooth balls. Leave to dry for 1 hour.
7. Temper the chocolate. Using your hands, roll the balls in the tempered chocolate.
8. Finally, roll the balls in cocoa powder. Put them in a sieve and shake off excess powder.

Tip
Chocolate truffle can be flavored with cinnamon, anise stars, licorice, tea or coffee powder boiled with cream and sieved. If you choose flavored liquor, use about 1 1/2 tbs and reduce the cream by the same amount.

Four Brothers   makes about 25

● ●

This classic chocolate candy, highlighting caramelized hazelnuts, is not only delicious but also quite easy to make. Spanish, or Italian hazelnuts from Piemonte, are my particular favorites.

7 oz (200 g) hazelnuts
2.5 oz (70 g) confectioners' sugar
1 tsp freshly squeezed lemon juice
1 hazelnut-sized knob of unsalted butter

For coating

7 oz (200 g) semisweet chocolate (Valrhona Caraque 56% or Marabou dark)

1. Preheat oven to 400°F. Place the nuts on a baking sheet and roast for about 10 minutes until golden brown, stirring occasionally.
2. Use a tea towel to rub off the skins. Separate the nuts from the skins.
3. Reduce oven to 212°F.
4. Using a large saucepan, stir the nuts over a strong heat. Add confectioners' sugar and lemon juice. Caramelize the nuts to a golden color, stirring continuously with a metal or wooden spoon.
5. Remove the saucepan and stir in the butter, until the nuts separate.
6. Spread out the nuts on a baking sheet covered with a baking cloth. Place in the oven, leaving the oven door open.
7. Place the nuts together in fours, as in the photo below. Leave to cool (if they stiffen too quickly heat them up again with the oven door shut).
8. Temper the dark chocolate; see p. 35. Using a fork, dip the nuts into the chocolate. Tap the fork on the edge of the bowl to remove any excess and prevent "feet" forming when the nuts are placed to harden on parchment paper.

Chocolate Toffee, p. 60, and Four Brothers.

Palet d'Or Pur Caraïbe   makes about 25

● ● ●

This classic French chocolate is made by all chocolatiers. It should melt on the tongue and is decorated with a piece of gold leaf. The best Palet d'Or I ever tasted was at Bernachons in Lyon.

The chocolate contains trinitario beans from Trinidad. Of course, it tastes just as good without gold leaf, but isn't it a beautiful decoration! (Gold leaf can be bought at frame makers.)

gold leaf, if you wish
1 sheet acetate film

Ganache

8.4 oz (240 g) bittersweet chocolate (Valrhona Grand Cru Pur Caraïbe 66.5% or Marabou dark)
5.6 oz (160 g) heavy cream (3/4 cup)
1.4 oz (40 g) honey
1.4 oz (40 g) unsalted butter, room temperature

For coating

7 oz (200 g) semisweet chocolate (Valrhona Caraque 56% or Marabou dark)

DAY 1
Make the ganache

1. Finely chop the chocolate and place in a microwave bowl.
2. Boil the honey and cream in a small saucepan. Pour the mixture over the chocolate and stir with a plastic spoon or hand blender into an even, pliable ganache.
3. Put the thermometer in the ganache. At 95–104°F, stir or mix in the butter.
4. Pour the ganache into small round plastic containers, about 0.4 oz (10 g) in each. Leave to firm for 24 hours, ideally at 54–59°F.

DAY 2

5. Place the containers in the refrigerator for 1 hour. Press out the ganache onto parchment paper and leave in room temperature for about 30 minutes.
6. Cut out 25 squares of acetate film, about 1 x 1 inch. Using the tip of a knife, put a piece of gold leaf on each square.
7. Temper the chocolate; see p. 35. Using a fork, dip the pieces into the chocolate. Smooth off the underside of the chocolate against the edge of the bowl and place on parchment paper. Take the acetate film, with the gold leaf downwards, and place on top of the chocolates.
8. Leave to harden in the refrigerator for 30 minutes before removing the film.

Bitter Chocolate Ganache Grand Cru Guanaja, recipe p. 51, and Palet d'Or Pur Caraïbe with gold leaf.

Côte d'Or makes about 30

● ● ●

I remember this classic chocolate candy from my time at Coba School in Switzerland. It has always been one of my favorites. The taste combination of black currants, marinated in sugar and rum, and dark chocolate is breathtaking! See photo, p. 83.

1 multi-cavity candy mold, oval or round shapes

Black currant fondant
1.8 oz (50 g) black currant purée, made from 5.3 oz (150 g) fresh or frozen berries
3.5 oz (100 g) water (1/2 cup)
8.8 oz (250 g) sugar
1.1 oz (30 g) glucose

For molding
7 oz (200 g) semisweet chocolate (Valrhona Caraque 56% or Marabou dark)
black currants, marinated in liquor; see p. 82
3.5 oz (100 g) milk chocolate (Valrhona Jivara Lactée 40% or Marabou milk chocolate)

1. Crush 5.3 oz (150 g) fresh or frozen black currants in a blender and pass through a strainer.
2. Pour the water into a small saucepan and add sugar. Heat slowly, to ensure the sugar dissolves properly.
3. Add glucose to the sugar syrup and boil to 280°F, or do a finger test; see p. 45.
4. Heat the black currant purée in another saucepan.
5. Add the purée to the sugar syrup and swirl the pan until thoroughly mixed.
6. Spread the mixture on a water-sprinkled marble slab, or draining board. Cool to about 95°F.
7. Work by hand, or use a spatula, until it begins to whiten (see Fondant/Peppermint Pastilles, p. 35).
8. Temper the semisweet chocolate and mold shells; see p. 36. Leave to harden.
9. Drain the marinated black currants in a colander and place one in each shell.
10. Heat the fondant to 82°F. Using a paper cone with a hole cut out of it, fill the shells 3/4 full with fondant. Leave overnight.
11. Heat up and temper the milk chocolate. Spread a thin layer over the molds and leave to harden for 30 minutes.
12. Knock out the candies onto parchment paper.

Earl Grey Ganache makes about 25

● ●

A refined method of flavoring ganache, using different kinds of tea, such as Earl Grey.

Tea ganache
0.3 oz (8 g) Earl Grey tea
1.4 oz (40 g) heavy cream (1/5 cup)
0.9 oz (25 g) heavy cream (1/8 cup)
8.1 oz (230 g) bittersweet chocolate (Valrhona Grand Cru Manjari 64.5% or Marabou dark)
1.1 oz (30 g) orange-flower honey
0.9 oz (25 g) unsalted butter, room temperature

For coating
7 oz (200 g) milk chocolate (Valrhona Jivara Lactée 40% or Marabou milk chocolate)

DAY 1
Make the tea ganache
1. Make tea, using 1.4 oz (40 g) boiling cream. Leave to brew for 5 minutes, strain the tea into a small saucepan and add the rest of the cream. Bring up the total amount of liquid to 5.8 oz (165 g). The tea can use up some of the cream, so adjust the cream you add accordingly.
2. Finely chop the dark chocolate and place in a plastic bowl.
3. Add honey to the tea-cream. Boil and pour over the chocolate. Mix with a plastic spoon or hand blender into a smooth and pliable ganache.
4. Put a thermometer in the ganache. At 95–104°F, mix in the butter.
5. Place in a foil container about 1/2 inch high, lined with parchment paper. Leave in a cool place, 54–59°F, for about 24 hours.

DAY 2
6. Chop and melt milk chocolate to 113°F, in a microwave oven or double boiler.
7. Pour about 2 tbs over the ganache and spread backwards and forwards until the chocolate begins to harden. Turn over the ganache.
8. Cut into 1 x 1 inch squares and temper the chocolate; see p. 35. Using a fork, dip the squares into the chocolate. Decorate with a diagonal line drawn across the chocolate.

Left: Earl Grey Ganache. Above: Arabica Ganache, p. 56. Below: Licorice Ganache, p. 56.

Arabica Ganache   makes about 40

• •

Coffee adds a wonderful flavor to ganache. See photo, p. 54.

Coffee ganache
0.4 oz (12 g) crushed Arabica coffee beans
4.6 oz (130 g) heavy cream (2/3 cup)
8.8 oz (250 g) bittersweet chocolate (Valrhona Grand Cru Guanaja 70.5% or Marabou dark)
1.4 oz (40 g) honey
1.2 oz (35 g) unsalted butter, room temperature

For coating
7 oz (200 g) semisweet chocolate (Valrhona Caraque 56% or Marabou dark)
coffee beans for decoration

DAY 1
Make the coffee ganache
1. Crush the coffee beans in a mortar. Boil the cream in a small saucepan and pour over the crushed coffee. Leave to brew for 5 minutes.
2. Finely chop the chocolate and place in a plastic bowl.
3. Sieve off the beans and pour the boiled cream into a saucepan. Add honey and re-boil the coffee-cream and pour over the chocolate. Using a spoon or hand blender, mix into a smooth and pliable ganache. Let cool to 95–104°F. Add butter and mix thoroughly.
4. Place the ganache in a 1/2 inch high foil container, lined with parchment paper. Leave in a cool place, 54–59°F, for 24 hours.

DAY 2
5. Melt the chocolate to 131°F and pour two tablespoons on the ganache. Spread backwards and forwards until the chocolate hardens. Use a ruler and knife to cut into 1 x 1 inch squares.
6. Temper the chocolate; see p. 35. Using a fork, dip squares of ganache into the chocolate. Scrape along the edge of the bowl to remove excess chocolate and prevent a "foot" forming when the squares are placed on parchment paper. Decorate with a coffee bean.

IMPORTANT!
Make sure the squares are at room temperature, 68°F, when dipping.

Licorice Ganache   makes about 30

• •

"Réglisse" should be available, packaged as granules, in most herb stores. Reglissé is concentrated licorice that can be used to flavor ice cream or candy. Here, it gives the ganache a robust but pleasant taste. See photo, p. 54.

1 sheet of bubble wrap

Ganache with licorice
7 oz (200 g) bittersweet chocolate (Valrhona Grand Cru Manjari 64.5% or Marabou dark)
2.6 oz (75 g) milk chocolate (Valrhona Jivara Lactée 40% or Marabou milk chocolate)
4.6 oz (130 g) heavy cream (2/3 cup)
1.4 oz (40 g) honey
0.4 oz (12 g) Reglissé granules (see above)
1.4 oz (40 g) unsalted butter

For coating
7 oz (200 g) milk chocolate (Valrhona Jivara Lactée or Marabou milk)

DAY 1
Make the ganache
1. Finely chop both the different kinds of chocolate and place in a microwave bowl.
2. Boil cream, honey and licorice whilst stirring. Mix smooth, using a hand blender. Bring back to the boil until the licorice has dissolved. Pour the mixture over the chocolate and mix with a plastic spoon into a smooth, pliable ganache.
3. Let cool to 95–104°F. Add butter and mix thoroughly. Transfer the ganache to a 1/2 inch high foil container and leave to firm in a refrigerator, or cool place at 54–59°F, for 24 hours.

DAY 2
4. Melt the chocolate for tempering. Put 2 tablespoonfuls on top of the ganache and spread backwards and forwards until the ganache stiffens. Cut out 1 x 1 inch squares, using a ruler. Make 30 squares of bubble wrap for an unusual decoration.
5. Temper the chocolate; see p. 35. Dip the squares, using a fork, and remove excess chocolate from the bottom before placing on parchment paper. Place a bubble wrap square on top of the chocolate and leave to harden in the refrigerator for about 30 minutes. Remove the bubble wrap, which will have made a fun pattern on the top.

Pistachio Marzipan Candy makes about 40

● ●

Pistachio nuts found in supermarkets are often not real pistachios. Real pistachios have an intense green color and a faint but pleasant aroma, which can be strengthened by adding orange-flower water.
See photo, p. 59.

Pistachio marzipan
2.6 oz (75 g) almonds
5.3 oz (150 g) pistachios, shelled
7.9 oz (225 g) sugar
3.5 oz (100 g) water (1/2 cup)
2.6 oz (75 g) glucose
1.8 oz (1/4 cup) Kirschwasser or Maraschino, or
    if you can't find these use rum
2 drops orange-flower water

For coating
10.5 oz (300 g) semisweet chocolate (Valrhona Caraque
    56% or Marabou dark)

1.8 oz (50 g) shelled pistachios, preferably from Sicily

DAY 1
Make the pistachio marzipan
1. Blanche the almonds. Leave to dry for 1 hour in a warm oven.
2. Pulverize the almonds and pistachios in a food processor or blender.
3. Mix sugar and cold water in a small saucepan. Boil and skim the surface with a tea strainer or similar.
4. Dip a small brush in water and wash down any sugar crystals that may form on the sides of the pan. Add glucose.
5. Boil the sugar syrup to 252°F. Check the temperature with a thermometer, or do a finger test (see p. 44).
6. Pour the sugar syrup onto the powdered nuts in the processor/blender and run for about 1 minute to make marzipan paste. Add Kirchwasser and orange-flower water, mixing thoroughly.
7. Scrape out the paste and cover with plastic wrap. Leave to mature overnight.

DAY 2
Roll out the paste and dip in the same way as walnut candy; see p. 58. Garnish with a pistachio.

Orange Marzipan makes about 40

●

See photo, p. 59.

5.6 oz (160 g) almonds
1.4 oz (40 g) preserved orange peel; see p. 82
5.3 oz (150 g) confectioners' sugar
1.4 oz (40 g) Grand Marnier (1/5 cup)

For coating
7 oz (200 g) semisweet chocolate (Valrhona Caraque 56%
    or Marabou dark)

1.8 oz (50 g) preserved orange peel, see p. 82, for
    decoration

DAY 1
1. Blanche the almonds and spread on a baking sheet. Dry for 1 hour, in a 212°F oven.
2. Finely chop the preserved orange peel.
3. Grind the almond and confectioners' sugar to a fine powder, in a food processor or blender.
4. Add the orange peel and Grand Marnier to the powder. Run for about 1 minute, to make marzipan paste.
5. Scrape out the paste and cover with plastic wrap. Leave to mature overnight.

DAY 2
6. Work the marzipan into a soft paste. Add more liquor if the marzipan feels too dry, or more sugar if the paste is too loose.
7. Roll out 2 equal lengths with the help of confectioners' sugar. Cut into 0.4 oz (10 g) pieces. Powdering your hands with confectioners' sugar, form the paste into small ovals. Leave to dry for 3 hours on parchment paper.
8. Cut preserved orange peel into thin strips and leave to dry for 3 hours.
9. Temper the chocolate; see p. 35. Using a fork, dip the marzipan and remove excess chocolate from the bottom to prevent a "foot" forming when placed on parchment paper.

Griotte Cherries   makes 30

•

A really wonderful taste! You can either conserve the cherries yourself, or buy them at the delicatessen. See photo, p. 63.

    30 preserved Griotte cherries; see p. 82, or bought
        French ones

    1 recipe fondant; see Peppermint Pastilles p. 74

For coating
    10.5 oz (300 g) semisweet chocolate (Valrhona Caraque
        56% or Marabou dark)

1. Place the cherries on a rack and drain and dry for about 3 hours.
2. Heat the fondant in a microwave oven or double boiler, stirring continuously until it reaches 158°F.
3. Dip the cherries in the fondant, leaving 1/2 inch of the stalk un-dipped. Place on parchment paper and leave to stiffen.
4. Temper the chocolate; see p. 35. Make a paper cone and fill 1/5 with chocolate. Pipe 30 round discs, about 1 inch diameter. Place a cherry on each disc and leave to harden.
5. Dip in the tempered chocolate, covering part of the stalk. Leave to harden.
6. Cut off the stalk to about 1/2 inch; see photo, p. 63.
7. After about 24 hours, the liqueur inside will be fluid.

Walnut Candy   makes about 40

• •

Walnut marzipan and dark chocolate make a tremendous combination. Flavor with honey and rum to heighten the taste experience.

Walnut marzipan
    3.5 oz (100 g) almonds
    3.5 oz (100 g) walnuts
    7 oz (200 g) sugar
    3.5 oz (100 g) water (1/2 cup)
    2.6 oz (75 g) honey
    1.8 oz (50 g) dark rum (1/4 cup)

For coating
    10.5 oz (300 g) semisweet chocolate (Valrhona Caraque
        56% or Marabou dark)

    7 oz (200 g) whole French walnuts for decoration

DAY1
Make the walnut marzipan
1. Blanche the almonds. Leave to dry for 1 hour in a 200°F oven.
2. Pulverize the almonds and walnuts in a blender.
3. Mix sugar and cold water in a small saucepan. Boil and skim the surface with a tea strainer or similar.
4. Dip a small brush in water and wash down any sugar crystals that may form on the sides of the pan.
5. Add honey and boil the sugar syrup to 252°F. Check the temperature with a thermometer, or do a finger test (see p. 44).
6. Pour the sugar syrup onto the powdered nuts in the mixer. Run for about 1 minute to make marzipan paste. Add the rum and mix thoroughly.
7. Scrape out the paste and cover with plastic wrap. Leave to mature overnight.

DAY 2
8. Using your hands, work the marzipan into a pliable paste. Add a few more drops of rum if the paste is too stiff.
9. Flouring the rolling pin with confectioners' sugar, roll out the marzipan, about 1/3 inch thick. Cut out small circles, using a cookie cutter dipped in confectioners' sugar. Place on parchment paper and leave for about 2 hours to stiffen.
10. Temper the chocolate; see p. 35. Dip the pieces in the chocolate, removing excess chocolate by scraping along the edge of the bowl. Place on parchment paper and decorate with a walnut. Leave to harden.

Pistachio Marzipan Candy, dipped and un-dipped, recipe p. 57.
Orange Marzipan Candy, dipped and un-dipped, recipe p. 57.
Walnut Marzipan Candy, dipped and un-dipped.

Chocolate Toffee   makes 30

• •

3.5 oz (100 g) heavy cream (1/2 cup)
5.3 oz (150 g) sugar
5.3 oz (150 g) honey
3.5 oz (100 g) bittersweet chocolate (Valrhona Grand Cru 70.5% or Marabou dark)

For coating

7 oz (200 g) semisweet chocolate (Valrhona Caraque 56% or Marabou dark)

DAY 1

1. Pour cream, sugar and honey in a small thick-bottomed saucepan. Bring to the boil, while stirring with a metal or wooden spoon.
2. Dip a small brush in water and wash down any sugar crystals that may form on the sides of the pan. Reduce heat and boil to 248°F, while stirring. Use a thermometer or do a finger test; see p. 44.
3. Finely chop chocolate and add to the mixture. Bring back to the boil and do a sauce test; see p. 44.
4. Pour the liquid toffee into a 3 1/4 inch wide foil container, lined with parchment paper. Leave to cool overnight.

DAY 2

5. Melt the chocolate; see p. 35. Pour about 2 tbs on the toffee. Spread the chocolate backwards and forwards until it hardens.
6. Using a serrated knife and ruler, cut into 1 x 1 inch squares.
7. Reheat the tempered chocolate. Using a fork, dip the squares into the chocolate. Scrape along the edge of the bowl to remove excess chocolate and prevent a "foot" forming when placed on parchment paper. Slash the surface diagonally with the fork to decorate.

The toffee is spread with non-tempered chocolate. See also photo p. 52.

Honold Grapes   makes 30

• •

Seedless green grapes come on to the market at the end of August. When I worked in Switzerland, we used to bottle the grapes in dark rum, add some vanilla pods, and store in a sunny place. When the grapes had darkened, they were ready for candy making. Sometimes the grapes would have to stand for a whole year before we could use them. You can conserve the grapes yourself using the same method. The grapes should be ready in time for making delicious Christmas candies. See photo on opposite page.

2.8 oz (80 g) confectioners' sugar
0.4 oz (10 g) real vanilla sugar
0.4 oz (10 g) potato flower
1 batch fondant; see Peppermint Pastilles, p. 74
30 preserved grapes

For coating

7 oz (200 g) semisweet chocolate (Valrhona Caraque 56% or Marabou dark)

1. Sieve confectioners' sugar, vanilla sugar and potato flour. Mix thoroughly and put aside.
2. Make the fondant; see Peppermint Pastilles, p. 74.
3. Place the grapes on a rack and leave for 2 hours to dry.
4. Put the fondant in a plastic bowl and heat to 158°F, in a microwave oven or using a double boiler.
5. Using a fork, dip the grapes into the fondant. Place on parchment paper and leave to stiffen.
6. Temper the chocolate; see p. 35. Using your hands, roll the grapes in chocolate. Leave to harden and repeat the procedure. Finally, roll the grapes in confectioners' sugar.
7. When the grapes have hardened, place them in a sieve and shake off excess sugar.

Drain off the preserved fruit. Honold Grapes, above and right.

Chocolate Beans   makes about 30

• •

Gianduia is the Italian word for a hazelnut candy from Piemonte. They are filled with a kind of soft nougat, consisting of confectioners' sugar and roasted hazelnuts. The sugar and nuts are mixed together until the nut oil is released, giving the paste a melting consistency. See photo, p. 65.

1 multi-cavity candy mold, preferably oval shapes

Hazelnut gianduia

3.5 oz (100 g) hazelnuts
1 tsp (5 g) Arabica coffee beans
2.1 oz (60 g) confectioners' sugar
1/2 vanilla pod
3.5 oz (100 g) milk chocolate (Valrhona Givara Lactée 40% or Marabou milk)

For molding

1.8 oz (50 g) bittersweet chocolate (Valrhona Manjari 64.5% or Marabou dark)
7 oz (200 g) white chocolate (Valrhona Ivoire, Lindt, Callebaut or Fazer)

1. Preheat oven to 400°F.
2. Spread out the nuts on a baking sheet. Roast for about 10 minutes until golden brown, stirring occasionally.
3. Use a tea towel to rub the skins off the nuts. Separate the skins from the nuts.
4. Put the skinned nuts in a blender or food processor. Add coffee beans and confectioners' sugar. Slice open the vanilla pod and scrape out the seeds.
5. Run in the blender for 5–10 minutes to make an oily, liquid paste, with a temperature of about 160°F.
6. Finely chop the chocolate and add to the paste. Run in the blender until the chocolate has melted. Pour out onto a marble slab or other cold surface, and temper (as chocolate).

Making candy molds, p. 36

7. When the filling has begun to stiffen, at about 80°F, use a pastry bag with a smooth no. 8 tip and pipe the candy molds 3/4 full. Leave to for 30 minutes until firm.
8. Heat up the chocolate left over from molding and temper. Spread a thin layer over the candy molds. Place in a refrigerator for 30 minutes to harden. Take out and knock the candies onto parchment paper.

Pineapple Tips   makes 36

•

You can buy preserved pineapple, but it's not as much fun as making it yourself!

3 slices preserved pineapple; see p. 82
1 batch fondant; see Peppermint Pastilles, p. 74

For coating

7 oz (200 g) semisweet chocolate (Valrhona Caraque 56% or Marabou dark)

1. Divide each pineapple slice into 12 pieces. Place on a rack and dry for at least 3 hours.
2. Heat the fondant to 158°F in a microwave oven, or double boiler, while stirring.
3. Dip the pineapple tips to 2/3 in the fondant. Leave to stiffen on parchment paper.
4. Temper the chocolate; see p. 35. Dip the tips into the chocolate leaving visible a rim of fondant. Leave to harden.

In the strainer, Honold Grapes (p. 60).
On the plate, from left: candied orange or lemon peel dipped in chocolate (p. 77),
Pineapple Tips, a Marron Glacé dipped in chocolate (p. 78) and Griotte Cherries (p. 58).

Almond Praline   makes about 30

• •

Praline filling is a classic in the world of chocolate confectionary. Caramelizing almonds or nuts gives off a heavenly smell. Scandinavians often call this soft nougat.

    3.5 oz (100 g) whole almonds, for decoration
    3.5 oz (100 g) almonds
    1/4 vanilla pod
    1.4 oz (40 g) water (1/5 cup)
    2.8 oz (80 g) sugar
    5.3 oz (150 g) milk chocolate (Valrhona Jivara Lactée 40% or Marabou milk)

For coating

    7 oz (200 g) milk chocolate (Valrhona Jivara Lactée 40% or Marabou milk)

DAY 1

1. Preheat oven to 400°F.
2. Blanche the almonds.
3. Keep the finest almonds for decoration.
4. Spread the almonds on a baking sheet. Roast for about 10 minutes to golden brown, stirring occasionally.
5. Divide the vanilla pod, scrape out the seeds and place in a 2-quart saucepan. Add water and sugar. Boil to 240°F, or do a finger test (see p. 44). Add the almonds and continue to boil until the almonds start to sputter and pop.
6. Stir until the sugar begins to turn white and "die." Caramelize to a golden color. Spread out over parchment paper and leave to cool.
7. Put the praline mixture in a blender and mix into an oily, liquid paste at 160°F. This takes about 5 minutes.
8. Finely chop the chocolate and add to the praline paste. Mix until the chocolate has melted.
9. Pour the praline paste onto a marble slab or other cold surface. Temper as chocolate.
10. When the chocolate begins to harden, at about 82°F, spread it in a 1/2 inch thick layer in a parchment-lined aluminum container. Cool at 55–60°F for 24 hours.

DAY 2

11. Melt the chocolate for coating. Pour about 2 tbs on the praline filling, spreading backwards and forwards until firm. Turn over and cut into 1 x 1 inch squares using a knife and ruler. Leave for about 20 minutes until the filling reaches room temperature.
12. Temper the chocolate; see p. 35. Using a fork, dip the squares in the chocolate, scraping the bottom against the side of the bowl to prevent a "foot" forming when placed on parchment paper. Decorate with a roasted almond; see photo below left.

Pyramids   makes 32

• •

Plastic pyramid molds should be available at a well-stocked kitchen or herb store.

    1 plastic mold, pyramid shapes

For molding

    0.9 oz (25 g) bittersweet chocolate (Valrhona Grand Cru Guanaja 70.5% or Marabou dark)
    7 oz (200 g) white chocolate (Valrhona Ivoire, Lindt, Callebaut or Fazer)

Anise star ganache

    1.8 oz (50 g) heavy cream (1/4 cup)
    0.4 oz (10 g) acacia honey
    2 anise stars
    4.2 oz (120 g) milk chocolate (Valrhona Jivara Lactée 40% or Marabou milk)
    0.5 oz (15 g) cognac (1 tbs)

Chocolate molding

1. Temper the dark chocolate; see p. 35. Dip a stiff brush into the chocolate, draw a knife across the brush and splash the inside of the molds.
2. Temper the white chocolate and mold the shells; see p. 37.

Anise star ganache

3. Boil together the cream, honey and anise stars. Leave for 10 minutes before removing the stars.
4. Finely chop the chocolate and place in a plastic container.
5. Re-boil the cream and pour over the chocolate. Stir with a plastic spoon into a smooth and pliable ganache.
6. Stir the cognac into the ganache. Leave to cool to 81–82°F.
7. 3/4 fill the shells with ganache, using a paper cone.
8. Leave to stiffen until a film has formed on the surface.
9. Temper the remaining chocolate and spread a thin covering layer over the molds. Place in a refrigerator for 30 minutes to harden. Knock out the candies from the mold onto parchment paper.

At the top: Pistachio Ganache (p. 50). From the left: Balsamic Ganache (p. 77), Chocolate Beans (p. 62) and Pyramids.

Classic Montelimar Egg, recipe p. 69.
In front: Pistachio Nougat, Chocolate Nougat and White Nougat.

Almond Splinters   makes about 30

●

This easy-to-make candy tastes even more scrumptious if you add some finely chopped orange zest to the almond mixture.

  5.3 oz (150 g) almonds
  1.4 (40 g) confectioners' sugar
  0.4 (10 g) Cointreau liqueur (2 tbs)
  3.5 oz (100 g) milk or bittersweet chocolate (Valrhona Jivara Lactée 40%, Valrhona Grand Cru Pur Caraïbe 66.5% or Marabou milk or dark chocolate)

1. Preheat oven to 400°F.
2. Blanche the almonds.
3. Cut the almonds lengthwise into splinters. Mix thoroughly with the confectioners' sugar and liqueur on a baking sheet. Roast for about 10 minutes until golden brown, stirring occasionally. Leave to cool.
4. Temper the chocolate; see p. 35. Add the almond splinters to the chocolate and mix well. Spoon out small, oval mounds of the mixture onto parchment paper.

Trianon   makes about 30

● ● ●

This wonderful crispy candy is worth all the patience required to make it. The shiny truffle and the crispy nougat taste quite delicious. Save this for a rainy winter day when you want to make something really special!

Milk ganache
  6 oz (170 g) milk chocolate (Valrhona Jivara Lactée 40% or Marabou milk)
  0.7 oz (20 g) egg yolk (1 yolk)
  1 oz (25 g) honey
  3.5 oz (100 g) heavy cream (1/2 cup)

Nougat
  2 oz (60 g) shredded almond
  8.8 oz (250 g) sugar
  2.6 oz (75 g) glucose
  1 tsp freshly squeezed lemon juice
  2.6 oz (75 g) unsalted butter, room temperature

For coating
  14 oz (400 g) semisweet chocolate (Valrhona Caraque 56% or Marabou dark)

Milk ganache
1. Finely chop the chocolate and place in a microwave bowl.
2. Whisk the egg yolk and honey until just frothy.
3. Boil the cream in a small saucepan and pour it over the egg yolk froth. Whisk together and pour back into the saucepan. Stir with a metal spoon over a low heat, until the mixture begins to thicken and reaches 185°F.
4. Finely strain the egg-cream mixture over the chocolate. Stir with a plastic spoon and hand blender, to a smooth and pliable ganache. Take out, cover with plastic wrap and leave to stiffen about 2 hours at room temperature.

Nougat
120 nougat discs are needed for 30 trianons.
5. Heat the oven to 400°F.
6. Spread the shredded almond on a baking sheet. Roast for about 5 minutes until golden brown, stirring often.
7. Use a rolling pin to finely crush the almond.
8. Spread the sugar on a baking sheet and heat in the oven for about 5 minutes.
9. Boil the glucose until golden brown. Add lemon juice and 1/3 of the sugar. Stir with a wooden spoon until the sugar melts and the nougat is light brown. Add the next 1/3 of the sugar and melt into the nougat, then the final 1/3. Stir in the butter and the almonds. Pour out onto a baking sheet and immediately roll out the nougat as thin as possible, using a rolling pin greased with cooking oil.
10. Roll out to a 1 inch thick sheet. If the nougat begins to stiffen, place it back in the oven on a baking cloth and heat for 5 minutes to re-soften.
11. Heat the nougat sheet for 5 minutes in the oven. Use a cookie cutter to make small discs. Let the nougat sheet cool before lifting out the discs.
12. Arrange 30 nougat discs on parchment paper.
13. Fill a plastic pastry bag with the ganache and pipe out 0.3 oz (8 g) balls. Place 3 nougat discs around each ball; see photo below.
14. Temper the chocolate; see p. 35. Using a fork, dip the truffles into the chocolate, removing the excess chocolate against the edge of the bowl. Leave to harden on parchment paper.

Assembling nougat discs around the ganache.

Montelimar Nougat makes about 80

• •

This nougat originated from the town of Montelimar in southern France. It's commonly known as French nougat here in Sweden. See photo, p. 65.

3.5 oz (100 g) hazelnuts
8.8 oz (250 g) almonds
4.4 oz (125 g) pistachios, shelled and skinned
3.5 oz (100 g) water
10.5 oz (300 g) sugar
6 oz (175 g) glucose
6 oz (175 g) honey
2 oz (60 g) egg white (2 whites)
1.8 oz (50 g) sugar
1 tbs freshly squeezed lemon juice

For coating
10.5 oz (300 g) semisweet chocolate (Valrhona Caraque 56% or Marabou dark)

DAY 1

1. Preheat oven to 400°F.
2. Spread the hazelnuts and almonds on a baking sheet and roast for about 10 minutes until golden brown. Rub off the skins and mix the kernels with the pistachios.
3. Pour the water in a 1-quart saucepan. Add sugar and whisk until it has melted completely. Boil up and skim with a tea strainer. Add glucose and honey and bring back to the boil.
4. Brush the inside edge of the pan with cold water to prevent crystallization.
5. When the sugar syrup is 250°F, begin to whisk the egg white, lemon juice and sugar until stiff.
6. Quickly heat the sugar syrup to 297°F. Use a thermometer, or do a finger test (see p. 44).
7. Whisking constantly, add the boiling sugar syrup to the egg white mixture. Blend slowly, by hand or using a blender, for about 5 minutes until the mixture begins to whiten.
8. Stirring vigorously, add the nuts and almonds. Spread the nougat over the draining board and leave to cool for 5 minutes. (If you add 1.8 oz (50 g) melted cocoa butter, the nougat will keep longer.)
9. Flour a rolling pin with confectioners' sugar and roll out the nougat, 1 inch thick, on parchment paper. Leave at room temperature overnight.

DAY 2

10. Cut into 1/2 inch wide lengths and divide these into 1 1/4 inch pieces.
11. Melt and temper the chocolate; see p. 35. Using a fork, dip the pieces in the chocolate, leaving the top uncovered.

Chocolate Nougat
Follow the recipe for Montelimar nougat but add 4.4 oz (125 g) dark chocolate.

Pistachio Nougat
Follow the recipe for Montelimar nougat but add an extra 1.8 oz (50 g) finely ground pistachio and 2 drops of orange-flower water.

Tip

Professionals often brush the topside with cocoa butter before dipping.

Above: Chocolate Log, p. 76. Below: chocolate discs decorated with nuts, p. 76.

Rigi Kirsch   makes 30

● ●

This Swiss candy symbolizes Mount Rigi, by the Luzern lake. It has a strong taste of Kirschwasser, which is a delicious flavoring for chocolate fillings, but other liquors can be substituted if preferred.

For coating
10.5 oz (300 g) semisweet chocolate (Valrhona Caraque 56% or Marabou dark)
1.8 oz (50 g) white chocolate (Valrhona Ivoire, Callebaut, Lindt or Fazer)

1.8 oz (50 g) unsalted butter, room temperature
4.4 oz (125 g) bittersweet chocolate (Valrhona Grand Cru Guanaja 70.5 % or Marabou dark)
1.8 oz (50 g) confectioners' sugar
1.8 oz (50 g) Kirschwasser or other liquor (1/4 cup)

1. Melt and temper the dark chocolate for coating; see p. 35. Pour the chocolate into a paper cone with a small hole at one end and pipe out 30 discs, about 1 inch diameter. Place on parchment paper and leave to harden.
2. Finely chop the chocolate and melt to 130°F.
3. Using 70°F butter, add confectioners' sugar and cream together. Add Kirschwasser and beat until light and fluffy.
4. Temper the chocolate; see p. 35. Add to the mixture and, using a baking spatula, work into a so-called butter truffle. Leave to stabilize for 5 minutes.
5. Put the truffle in a pastry bag and pipe out crests onto the chocolate discs. Leave to stiffen for 1 hour.
6. Heat the rest of the dark chocolate and re-temper. Dip the candies carefully scraping the bottom to remove excess chocolate.
7. Temper the white chocolate. Pour into a small paper cone. Cut a hole in the end and pipe a small amount over each candy. Leave to harden.

Chestnut Ganache, on the left and Rigi Kirsch.

Liqueur Bottles   makes about 20

● ● ●

Everyone can surely remember the sensation when the sugar crust breaks and floods your mouth with liqueur! The Frenchman Vernaut discovered the technique of making chocolate liqueurs in the 1850s. The combination of liqueur and chocolate is sensational. It is not too difficult to make liqueur bottles if you use a sugar thermometer.

Confectioners mold the bottles in powder boxes filled with warm starch. The mold impressions are made using a wooden strip with bottle shapes glued to it. The choice of liquor or liqueur is yours, but the alcoholic content should not be less than 40% or the sugar crust will be too weak.

35 oz (1000 g) cornstarch
3.5 oz (100 g) water (1/2 cup)
8.8 oz (250 g) sugar
2.6 oz (75 g) cognac (1/3 cup)

The warm cornstarch is sifted over the molded bottles.

For coating
7 oz (200 g) semisweet chocolate (Valrhona Caraque 56% or Marabou dark)

DAY 1

1. Preheat oven to 175°F. Spread the cornstarch on a baking sheet and dry for at least 12 hours in the oven.
2. Sift the cornstarch through a fine sieve into a foil container. Stir with a whisk and smooth off the top with a ruler. Press the bottles into the starch to make a deep impression. Make as many impressions as possible in the container, and replace in the oven while you are making the sugar syrup.
3. Measure the water into a small saucepan and add sugar. Whisk continuously until the sugar has dissolved. Bring to the boil and skim thoroughly.
4. Wash the inside edge of the saucepan, using a brush dipped in cold water, to prevent crystallization.
5. When the sugar syrup has reached 246°F, remove the saucepan. Add the liquor and pour into another bowl. Swirl rigorously to ensure that the liquor and sugar syrup are properly mixed. Swirling also helps speed up crystallization of the sugar crust.

6. Return to the saucepan, cover with a moistened tea towel and leave to swell for 5–10 minutes.
7. Carefully pour the sugar syrup into the bottle impressions. Sift over with cornstarch to prevent the syrup thickening.
8. After 6 hours, carefully turn the bottles over and leave overnight to crystallize on the other side.

DAY 2

9. Remove the bottles carefully, brushing of excess starch.
10. Temper the chocolate; see p. 35. Dip the bottles carefully in the chocolate and remove excess chocolate on the edge of the saucepan. Leave to harden on parchment paper.

Useful tip
You can buy ready-made plaster molds, or use a bottle-shaped candy, glue it onto a cork and use that for making mold impressions. Readymade chocolate liqueur bottles can also be used.

Leftover cornstarch can be used many times but must be heated properly before use.

The cornstarch is brushed off the liqueur bottles. The chocolate-coated bottles are on the right.

Large Chestnuts   makes about 20

• •

This is an autumn specialty, which I always used to make when I worked at the Hollandia bakery in Malmö. They were very popular in those days, and I see that they still make them!

Royal icing, or "glacé royale," originated in France when a baker discovered a way of grinding sugar to a powder and whipping it with egg white, and a little lemon juice, into a glaze that would stiffen. The baker built the whole Bordeaux cathedral with this icing and a new recipe was born!

1 batch pistaschio marzipan; see p. 57.

Hazelnut gianduia
5.5 oz (150g) hazelnuts
3.5 oz (100 g) confectioner's sugar
5.5 oz (150 g) bittersweet chocolate (Valrhona Grand Cru Guanaja 70.5% or Marabou dark)
7 oz (200 g) semisweet chocolate (Valrhona Caraque 56% or Marabou dark)

Icing
3.5 oz (100 g) confectioner's sugar
1 oz (30 g) egg white (about 1)
1 tsp newly squeezed lemon juice

DAY 1
Make 1 batch pistaschio marzipan; see p. 57.

DAY 2
Hazelnut gianduia
1. Preheat oven to 400°F.
2. Roast the nuts for about 10 minutes on a baking sheet, stirring occasionally.
3. Using a tea towel, rub the skins from the nuts. Place the nuts and confectioner's sugar in a food processor and mix to an oily liquid paste. The paste is ready when it has reached 160°F.
4. Finely chop the chocolate and add to the paste. Mix until the chocolate has melted. Pour the paste onto a marble slab or other cold surface. Let cool during tempering, just as with chocolate.
5. When the paste has firmed, roll it into 2 lengths with a rolling pin floured with confectioner's sugar. Cut the lengths into 20 pieces and form them into balls. Leave to stiffen on parchment paper for about 1 hour.
6. Temper the chocolate; see p. 35. Using a fork, dip the balls. Tap the fork on the edge of the bowl to remove excess chocolate. Leave to harden.
7. Roll out the marzipan until about 1/4 inch thick. Press out circles using a cookie cutter (1/4 inch diameter). You will need 2 for each chestnut.
8. Brush the circles with a little Kirschwasser or other liquor. Fold the marzipan like a shell around the chestnut, leaving a section open (see on opposite page).

Royal icing
9. Finely sift the confectioner's sugar and pour into a clean metal bowl. Add egg white and lemon juice and whisk into frothy icing. Cover the bowl with plastic wrap so it does not dry out. Put a tablespoon of the icing into a small paper cone, cut a hole in the bottom and pipe small "spikes" on the marzipan shell.
10. Splash some red artificial coloring, using a stiff brush and knife, on the open part of the chestnut. Many pastry chefs finally spray the chestnuts with melted cocoa butter.

Chestnuts, recipe on this page.

Peppermint Pastilles   makes about 50

• •

"Fondant"—which means melting—was invented by a French pastry chef in the mid-19th century. Fondant can be used for glazing, pastilles and nougat.

Fondant

  3.5 oz (100 g) water (1/2 cup)
  9 oz (250 g) sugar
  2 oz (50 g) glucose
  5 drops peppermint oil

  3.5 oz (100 g) bittersweet chocolate (Valrhona Grand Cru Guanaja 70.5% or Marabou dark)

Fondant

1. Measure the water into a 1-quart saucepan. Whisk in the sugar until fully dissolved.
2. Place the saucepan over a low heat. Leave until the sugar has dissolved and the sugar syrup begins to boil. Using a brush dipped in cold water, wash down any crystals that may form on the sides of the pan. Skim with a tea strainer.
3. Add glucose and continue to brush the inside of the saucepan.
4. Boil to 244°F. Use a thermometer or do a finger test; see p. 44.
5. Cool the saucepan, in a bowl of cold water, to halt boiling. Take out and dry the underside of the saucepan.
6. Pour the sugar syrup onto a water-sprinkled surface, preferably a marble slab or a clean draining board. Sprinkle the sugar syrup with cold water to prevent a crust forming.
7. Leave to cool for 5 minutes. Work with a spatula until the glaze whitens.
8. Put the glaze in a glass jar, sprinkle the surface with water, and cover with a tight lid.

The fondant is tabled until it whitens.

Molding pastilles

9. Heat the fondant to 165°F in a microwave oven. Add peppermint oil and stir.
10. Pour into a paper cone, cut a hole in the bottom and pipe out 1 1/4 inch sized discs on parchment paper. Leave to harden at room temperature.
11. Temper the chocolate; see p. 35. Fill a paper cone, make a small hole and pipe a drop of chocolate on each disc. Leave to harden.

Chocolate Almonds   makes about 60

•

Chocolate almonds are a "must" on my Christmas table! You can also use hazelnuts or new-roasted coffee beans. If using coffee beans, increase the amount of sugar to 1.4 oz (40 g).

  3.5 oz (100 g) almonds
  1 oz (25 g) confectioner's sugar
  1 tsp freshly squeezed lemon juice
  1 pat butter
  7 oz (200 g) bittersweet chocolate (Valrhona Grand Crue Guanaja 70.5%)
  1 oz (25 g) cocoa powder, preferably Valrhona

1. Preheat oven to 400°F.
2. Spread the un-blanched almonds on a baking sheet. Roast for 10 minutes until golden brown, stirring occasionally. Put the almonds in a small saucepan with confectioners' sugar and lemon juice. Caramelize to golden brown, stirring constantly.
3. Remove the saucepan from the stove. Add the pat of butter and stir until the almonds separate. Place the almonds on parchment paper and leave to cool.
4. Temper the chocolate; see p. 35. Place the almonds in a metal bowl. Pour over about 1/3 of the chocolate and stir until the almonds have separated. Repeat this 3 times or until the chocolate is used up and the almonds are fully coated. Leave to harden between each coating.
5. Place the almonds on parchment paper and sift over with cocoa powder. Stir the almonds around to ensure they are fully coated.
6. Place the almonds in a sieve and shake to remove excess cocoa powder.

Chocolate Almonds; see opposite page.

Chocolate Logs makes about 35

• •

This delicious nut and almond flavor is best suited to milk chocolate.

> 1 batch pistaschio marzipan; see p. 57
> 1 batch hazelnut gianduia; see p. 62
> 7 oz (200 g) milk chocolate (Valrhona Jivara Lactée 40% or Marabou milk chocolate)

DAY 1
Make a batch of pistaschio marzipan; see p. 57.

DAY 2
Make a batch hazelnut gianduia; see p. 62.

1. Knead the gianduia until pliable. Divide into four pieces, and roll them into lengths of 3/4 inch diameter on parchment paper. Leave to stiffen.
2. Roll out the marzipan to about 1/4 inch thick, to the same length as the gianduia.
3. Brush the marzipan with a little cognac. Envelope the gianduia lengths in the pistaschio paste. Cutting off any excess of pistaschio paste at the join.
4. Allow the lengths to dry somewhat. Roll them to keep their shape.
5. Melt and temper the chocolate; see p. 35. Brush the lengths with chocolate and leave to stiffen. Turn the lengths over and brush on the other side.
6. Cut up small pieces of chocolate log with a sharp knife. You can see the result on p. 68.

Nutty Chocolate Discs makes about 25

•

These make excellent goodies for guests. Use whichever kind of chocolate you like best, or mix them.

> 1.8 oz (50 g) hazelnuts, roasted and peeled
> 1.8 oz (50 g) walnuts
> 1.8 oz (50 g) macadamia nuts
> 1.8 oz (50 g) pistaschios
> candied orange peel, raisins or pine kernels for decoration
> 7 oz (200 g) dark, white or milk chocolate

1. Preheat oven to 400°F. Roast the hazelnuts for 10 minutes until golden brown. Stirring occasionally. Use a tea towel to rub off the peel.
2. Temper the chocolate; see p. 35. Using a paper cone, cut a hole in the bottom and pipe out 1 1/4 inch sized discs of chocolate. Place the nuts on the chocolate discs and decorate with raisins or candied orange peel if you wish. Leave to harden; see photo, p. 68.

Nutmegs with Cinnamon and Honey Ganache makes about 30

• •

A fantastic candy, formed like a nutmeg and with a flavor clash of chocolate, cinnamon and honey. The most delicious cinnamon ganache I ever ate was made by Paul Hevin, the Parisian chocolatier. He has four stores in Paris, the best of which is on the Place Vendôme.

Ganache
> 4.4 oz (125 g) milk chocolate (Valrhona Jivara Lactée 40% or Marabou milk chocolate)
> 4.4 oz (125 g) bittersweet chocolate (Valrhona Grand Cru Guanaja 70.5% or Marabou dark)
> 2.8 oz (80 g) heavy cream (1/3 cup)
> 1 tsp (5 g) pale, whole cinnamon from Sri Lanka, can be found in a herb store.
> 1.8 oz (50 g) honey
> 2 tsp (10 g) dark rum

For coating
> 7 oz (200 g) milk chocolate (Valrhona Jivara Lactée 40% or Marabou milk chocolate)
> 1.8 oz (50 g) cocoa powder, preferably Valrhona

DAY 1
Make the ganache

1. Finely chop the chocolate.
2. Boil the cream, cinnamon and honey in a small saucepan. Remove from the heat and cover with a lid. Leave to draw for 10 minutes.
3. Remove the cinnamon sticks. Bring the mixture back to the boil and pour over the chopped chocolate. Stir into a smooth and pliable ganache.
4. Put the ganache in a shallow dish and cover with plastic wrap. Leave to stiffen for about 4 hours at room temperature.
5. Using a pastry bag with a smooth no. 10 tip, pipe out small balls of ganache, about 0.4 oz (10 g). (Use scales to check the size.)
6. Place in a refrigerator to stiffen for about 30 minutes. Sift over with cocoa powder and form into nutmeg shapes. Leave on parchment paper to stiffen overnight.

DAY 2
7. Melt and temper the chocolate; see p. 35. Using your hands, roll the nutmegs in the chocolate and leave to harden.
8. Dip the nutmegs in the chocolate, using a fork. Place them on a plate of cocoa powder.
9. Make lengthwise furrows in the nutmegs by rolling them over a fork. Leave in the cocoa powder to harden.
10. Put the nutmegs in a colander and sieve off excess cocoa powder.

Balsamic Ganache　　　makes about 25

● ●

Balsamic vinegar makes a stunning flavoring for ganache. See photo, p. 65.

1 multi-cavity candy mold, ball shapes

For molding
    7 oz (200 g) white chocolate (Valrhona Ivoire, Lindt,
        Callebaut or Fazer)
    1.8 oz (50 g) bittersweet chocolate (Valrhona Grand Cru
        Manjari 64.5% or Marabou dark)

Ganache
    4.9 oz (140 g) bittersweet chocolate (Valrhona Grand Cru
        Manjari 64.5% or Marabou dark)
    2.1 oz (60 g) quality balsamic vinegar (1/4 cup)
    3.5 oz (100 g) heavy cream (1/2 cup)
    2.5 oz (70 g) milk chocolate (Valrhona Jivara Lactée 40%
        or Marabou milk chocolate)
    8.8 oz (250 g) orange-flower honey
    1.4 oz (40 g) unsalted butter

Chocolate molding; see p. 37

Make the ganache
1. Finely chop the chocolate
2. Pour the vinegar in a small saucepan and boil until 0.9 oz
   (25 g) remains.
3. Add cream and honey. Bring back to the boil and pour the
   mixture over the chocolate. Mix with a plastic spoon, or hand
   blender, to a smooth and pliable ganache.
4. Cool to 95–104°F, add butter while stirring vigorously.
5. When the ganache is 81–82°F, put it in a pastry bag. Pipe out
   3/4 of the ganache into the chocolate molds. Leave in a cool
   place, 54–59°F, to stiffen.

6. Heat and temper (see p. 35) the chocolate left over from the
   molding. Pour a layer of chocolate over the molds and smooth
   off using a spatula. Leave in a refrigerator for 30 minutes to
   harden.
7. Knock the candies out of the molds.

Chocolate Coated Orange or Lemon Peel

●

See photo, p. 63.

    8 pieces preserved orange peel; see p. 80–82
    7 oz (200 g) bittersweet chocolate (Valrhona Grand Cru
        Guanaja 70.5% or Marabou dark)

DAY 1
1. Make a batch of preserved orange or lemon peel; see recipe
   p. 82. Save any unused peel. Properly preserved peel can keep
   in a refrigerator for several years.
2. Leave 8 lengths of peel on a rack to drain and dry overnight.

DAY 2 OR LATER
3. Cut the peel into 1/2 inch wide pieces.
4. Temper the chocolate; see p. 35.
5. Using a fork, dip the peel in the chocolate and place on
   parchment paper to harden.

Tip

Lemon and grapefruit peel is also excellent for preserving, candying and coating in chocolate!

Marron Glacé

● ●

I have a very special relationship with this continental specialty! The chestnuts can be conserved during the autumn and used for Christmas or New Year candies. You can also use them chopped in ice cream or parfait. They will keep for several years.

35 oz (1000 g) chestnuts

DAY 1
9 cups water
1 tsp sea salt
0.4 oz (10 g) alum, available
     at drugstores
2 vanilla pods
14 oz (400 g) sugar
2 3/4 cups water

DAY 2
5 oz (140 g) sugar

Chestnut glacé
4.4 oz (125 g) confectioners' sugar
1.4 oz (40 g) water (1/5 cup)
1 tsp freshly squeezed lemon juice

For coating
7 oz (200 g) semisweet chocolate (Valrhona Caraque 56%
     or Marabou dark)

DAY 3
4 oz (120 g) sugar

DAY 4
4 oz (120 g) sugar

DAY 5
4 oz (120 g) sugar
2.5 oz (75 g) honey

The glazed chestnuts left to cool on a rack.

DAY 1
1. Preheat oven to 400°F. Choose uniformly sized chestnuts. Make an incision and place them in a 4-quart ovenproof dish. Bake for 10 minutes or until tender.
2. Place the chestnuts in cold water and remove the outer shell, using a small knife. Carefully scrape and rinse the kernels.
3. Boil water, salt and alum. Let the chestnuts simmer until they are completely soft. Test with a needle.
4. Place some ice cubes in the water and remove from the heat to prevent the chestnuts boiling to pieces.
5. Place the chestnuts in a 5-quart glass bottle. Slice the vanilla pods lengthwise and place them in the bottle.
6. Boil sugar and water. Pour into the bottle and seal immediately. Leave to cool and store in a refrigerator.

DAY 2
7. Strain the sugar syrup, from the bottle, into a saucepan and add 5 oz (140 g) sugar. Re-boil and pour back into the bottle. Seal immediately and leave to cool. Store in the refrigerator.

DAY 3 AND DAY 4
Repeat the procedure from day 2, using 4 oz (120 g) sugar.

DAY 5
8. Pour the sugar syrup and chestnuts into a large saucepan. Add sugar and honey and bring to the boil. Skim off well and pour into clean glass bottles and seal immediately. Leave to cool and store in the refrigerator.
9. Preheat oven to 100°F. Place 20 chestnuts on an oven rack and dry in the oven for 60 minutes.

Chestnut glacé
10. Preheat oven to 350°F.
11. Mix confectioners' sugar and freshly squeezed lemon juice. Heat up and boil for about 1 minute. Pour half of the mixture onto a marble slab. Using a scraper, work the mixture until it begins to whiten (see fondant for Peppermint Pastilles, p. 74). Scrape the sugar mixture back into the saucepan and stir to a milky glaze. Using a fork, dip the chestnuts in the glacé and place on a rack.
12. Bake in the oven for about 2 minutes, until small sugar bubbles appear on the surface. Take out and cool.
    We have now glacéd the chestnuts, which can be kept for several months. They can be eaten with a glass of wine, though I prefer them coated in chocolate, of course!
13. Temper the chocolate; see p. 35. Using a fork, dip the chestnuts, removing excess chocolate to prevent a "foot" forming underneath. Place on parchment paper and leave to harden.

Useful tip
The addition of salt and alum prevents the chestnuts breaking up so easily when boiled.

Christmas Marzipan

●●

If you make your own marzipan you will avoid artificial preservatives. I flavor with vanilla and some bitter almonds to give my marzipan more character.

 0.4 oz (10 g) bitter almonds
 10.5 oz (300 g) almonds
 8.8 oz (250 g) sugar
 1/2 cup water
 3.5 oz (100 g) glucose
 1 vanilla pod

DAY 1

1. Blanche the almonds. Leave to dry overnight, or for 1 hour in a 200°F oven.
2. Pulverize the almonds in a blender or food processor.
3. Mix sugar and cold water in a small saucepan. Bring to the boil and skim the surface.
4. Use a brush dipped in water to wash down any sugar crystals that may form on the inside of the pan.
5. Add glucose, and boil the sugar syrup to 244°F. Use a sugar thermometer or do a finger test; see p. 44.
6. Pour the sugar syrup over the powdered almonds in the blender. Mix for about 1 minute into a paste.
7. Scrape out the marzipan paste. Cover in plastic wrap and leave to mature overnight.

DAY 2

8. Slice open the vanilla pods and scrape out the seeds. Work them into the marzipan paste.

Marzipan Pigs or "Smoked Eels" coated in chocolate

"Smoked eels" were a specialty at Braun's patisserie on Gustav Adolf Square in Malmö.

 14 oz (400 g) marzipan
 7 oz (200 g) dark chocolate (Valrhona Caraque 56% or
 Marabou dark)

DAY 1

Pig

1. Weigh 7 oz (200 g) marzipan and form into a pig's body.
2. Weigh three 0.5 oz (15 g) pieces and form two as ears and one as the tail. Attach to the body, as in the photo.
3. Leave to dry overnight at room temperature.

Smoked Eel

Roll out 7 oz (200 g) marzipan into a long, straight "eel". Leave to dry overnight at room temperature.

DAY 2

Melt and temper the chocolate; see p. 35. Place the pig and eel on a rack. Pour over the chocolate and shake the rack to ensure that the chocolate runs down properly. Lift off with a palette knife and place on parchment paper. Leave to harden.

> ### Useful tip
> *The marzipan must dry for 24 hours or the chocolate may crack.*

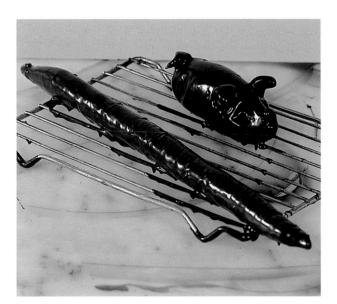

Lift the chocolate-dipped marzipan from the rack before the chocolate has hardened.

About preserving

Make sure all the fruit is properly blanched and soft when the sugar syrup is poured over them, otherwise the fruit will not suck in the liquid. By increasing the amount of sugar each day, the fruit swells up and absorbs the sugar. This technique can be used for most fruit. Ginger, for example, must be boiled for about 1 hour before it gets soft. Thin slices of candied ginger, coated in bittersweet chocolate, are known as Herrenpralin in Germany.

Preserved and marinated fruit and berries, p. 82.

Preserved and marinated fruit and berries

Marinated grapes

17.5 oz (500 g) seedless green grapes, preferably Thompson
5.3 oz (150 g) sugar
1 cup dark rum
1 vanilla pod

1. Rinse the grapes, and let them dry.
2. Place the grapes in a 5-quart glass bottle. Whisk the sugar and rum together and pour over the grapes.
3. Slice the vanilla pod lengthwise and place in the bottle. Seal immediately.
   The grapes should be stored for at least 3 months to become yellow and mature in flavor. Turn the bottles occasionally to melt the sugar. The grapes can be stored for several years and get better all the time.

Marinated cherries

Use the same recipe as for grapes but use Morello cherries instead. Gently prick the cherries before marinating. Use a good cognac instead of rum.

Marinated black currants or raspberries

17.5 oz (500 g) raspberries or black currants
9 oz (250 g) sugar
1 cup dark rum for black currants
1 cup raspberry schnapps for raspberries

Place the berries in a 2-quart glass bottle. Mix the sugar and rum or schnapps and pour into the bottle. Leave to marinate for at least 3 days. The taste improves with time. Can be stored for several months.

Preserved orange peel

DAY 1

35 oz (1000 g) oranges
1 vanilla pod
14 oz (400 g) sugar
2 3/4 cups water

DAY 2

5 oz (140 g) sugar

DAY 3

4 oz (120 g) sugar

DAY 4

4 oz (120 g) sugar

DAY 5

4 oz (120 g) sugar
2.5 oz (75 g) honey

DAY 1

1. Brush the oranges carefully, under running water.
2. Cut into 4 pieces and remove the peel.
3. Squeeze out the orange juice and keep if you wish.
4. Place the orange peel in a saucepan and cover with water.
5. Boil and let the peel simmer for 30 minutes, or until soft.
6. Add cold water to halt boiling.
7. Put the peel on to a cutting board and remove the white pith.
8. Rinse the zest in cold water. Leave to drain and dry.
9. Pack closely in clean 5-quart glass bottles.
10. Divide the vanilla pod lengthwise and place amongst the zests.
11. Boil up sugar and water and pour into the bottle. Allow to cool. Seal and store the bottles in a refrigerator.

DAY 2

12. Strain the sugar syrup from the bottle into a saucepan. Add 5 oz (140 g) sugar and bring to the boil. Pour back into the bottle and leave to cool. Seal and store in a refrigerator.

DAY 3–4

13. Repeat the procedure from day 2, using 4 oz (120 g) sugar.

DAY 5

14. Pour the zests and sugar syrup into a large saucepan. Add 4 oz (120 g) sugar and bring to the boil. Skim well, and add honey. Pour back into a sterilized bottle and leave to cool.

Tip
You can also use lemon and pink grapefruit peel for preserving.

Preserved pineapple, for candy

Del Monte pineapple slices are of good quality and do not need to be blanched, as fresh pineapple would.

DAY 1

1 can (28 oz) Del Monte pineapple slices, in their own juice
14 oz (400 g) sugar
2 3/4 cups water

DAY 2

5 oz (140 g) sugar

DAY 3

4 oz (120 g) sugar

DAY 4

4 oz (120 g) sugar

DAY 5

4 oz (120 g) sugar
2.5 oz (75 g) honey

DAY 1

1. Drain the pineapple slices and place them in a 3-quart glass bottle.
2. Boil up sugar and water and pour over the slices. Allow to cool, seal and refrigerate overnight.

DAY 2

3. Strain the sugar syrup into a saucepan. Add 5 oz (140 g) sugar and bring back to the boil. Pour over the pineapple slices and allow to cool. Seal and refrigerate overnight.

DAY 3–4

4. Repeat procedure from day 2, using 4 oz (120 g) sugar.

DAY 5

5. Put the pineapple slices and sugar syrup in a large saucepan. Add 4 oz (120 g) sugar and bring to the boil. Skim well and add honey. Pour into a clean glass jar. Leave to cool.

Raspberry Diamonds, p. 50 and Côte D'or, p. 55.

CHAPTER 5

chocolate cookies

The French called them petits fours sec, that is, dry cookies. Petits fours and coffee are an excellent way to round off a good meal. They should melt in your mouth and have a buttery tang. Always use real butter when baking this kind of cookie.

Useful tips for baking cookies

Always use butter that is at room temperature. This makes the butter easier to mix with other ingredients.

Use ordinary all-purpose flour, with low protein content. A proportion of the flour can be replaced by other gluten-free alternatives, such as potato flour or corn flour, to give a sandier texture.

Eggs are effective binders and also flavor heighteners.

Granulated sugar is usually used for baking cookies. Confectioners' sugar gives a more sandy and melting consistency, while granulated sugar gives a harder, crispier cookie. Raw sugar, brown sugar and cassonade sugar all give exciting flavor combinations. Sometimes a so-called propellant is used to make the dough lighter. Hartshorn salt is used for "dreams" to make them porous. Bicarbonate is used to give ginger biscuits their color. Baking powder can also be used in certain cookies.

The baking temperature for most cookies is usually between 350°F and 400°F. However, for cookies that contain a lot of sugar, the temperature should be 300°F or else they will deflate.

Chocolate Tuiles, p. 92

Brown almond flour

Pulverize un-blanched almonds in a blender or food processor, and sieve finely.

White almond flour

Blanch the almonds. Leave to dry overnight, or on a baking sheet in a 200°F oven for about 1 hour. Pulverize the almonds in a blender or food processor, and sieve finely.

TPT

You can make flour out of all sorts of nuts. "TPT" in a recipe means that the nut or almond flour should be mixed with an equal amount of granulated sugar before use. Tant pour tant (TPT) means the same amounts of both. Just as in marzipan, the mixture is 50% nuts and 50% sugar. 50/50 is a good rule of thumb in recipes.

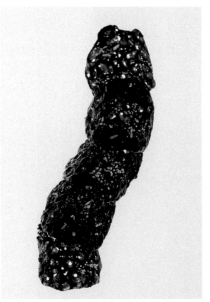

Chocolate Diamonds

makes about 40

•

See photo, p. 90.

7 oz (200 g) unsalted butter, room temperature
2.8 oz (80 g) confectioners' sugar
0.7 oz (20 g) egg yolk (about 1 yolk)
7 oz (200 g) all-purpose flour
0.9 oz (25 g) cocoa powder, preferably Valrhona.
1.4 oz (40 g) egg yolk (about 2 yolks)
1.8 oz (50 g) sugar

1. Mix the butter with confectioners' sugar and 0.7 oz (20 g) egg yolk.
2. Sieve together the flour and cocoa powder and add to the egg mixture.
3. Work all the ingredients into dough by hand or in a food processor. Divide the dough into 2 pieces. Roll out each piece into 16 inch lengths, using a floured rolling pin.
4. Place the lengths in the freezer for 30 minutes.
5. Brush the lengths with the beaten egg yolks and roll them in sugar. Return to the freezer.
6. Preheat oven to 350°F.
7. Cut the lengths of dough into 0.4 oz (11 g) slices.
8. Place the slices on parchment covered baking sheets and bake for 10–12 minutes, until golden brown.

New York, New York Brownies

makes about 40

•

See photo, p. 90

4.2 oz (120 g) bittersweet chocolate (Valrhona Grand Cru Guanaja 70.5% or Marabou dark)
4.2 oz (120 g) unsalted butter, room temperature
5.3 oz (150 g) walnuts
3.5 oz (100 g) raw sugar
1/2 tsp (2 g) salt
3.5 oz (100 g) confectioners' sugar
3.5 oz (100 g) egg (about 2 eggs)
4.2 oz (120 g) all-purpose flour
1 tsp (5 g) pure vanilla sugar

1. Finely chop the chocolate and melt in a microwave oven or double boiler, stirring continuously, until it reaches 131°F.
2. Add the unsalted butter and stir until melted.
3. Coarsely chop the walnuts and add. Stir until the batter is smooth.
4. Preheat oven to 425°F.
5. Spread the batter, about 1 inch thick, on a greased baking sheet. Bake for 6–8 minutes and leave to cool on the baking sheet.
6. Cut into 8 x 8 inch squares, using a sharp knife.

When I was working on board the Queen Elizabeth II liner, we used to serve these brownies cut into large pieces, with a scoop of vanilla ice cream and hot chocolate sauce. Scrumptious!

Chocolate Chip Cookies

makes about 60

●

I have chosen Valrhona Grand Cru Guanaja. This contains 70.5% cocoa and has an intense, slightly bitter taste which makes these cookies a little less sweet. We used this recipe on board M/S Vistafjord and our passengers loved them. We could bake endless quantities!

  3.5 oz (100 g) unsalted butter, room temperature
  1.8 oz (50 g) confectioners' sugar
  3.5 oz (100 g) raw sugar
  1.8 oz (50 g) egg (about 1 egg)
  7 oz (200 g) all-purpose flour
  1 tsp (5 g) bicarbonate
  1 tsp (5 g) vanilla sugar
  5.3 oz (150 g) bittersweet chocolate (Valrhona Grand Cru
      Guanaja 70.5% or Marabou dark)
  5.3 oz (150 g) pecan nuts

1. Mix together the butter, egg and both kinds of sugar.
2. Sieve the flour, bicarbonate and vanilla sugar, add to the mixture and work into dough.
3. Coarsely chop the nuts and chocolate and mix into the dough.
4. Divide the dough into 4 equal pieces and roll into 16 inch lengths.
5. Freeze the lengths for 30 minutes.
6. Preheat oven to 350°F.
7. Cut the lengths of dough into 0.4 oz (11 g) slices.
8. Place the slices on parchment covered baking sheets and bake for 12–14 minutes, until golden brown.

Brussels Cookies

makes about 60

●

This wonderful, melting dough is known as sablé in France. See photo, p. 90.

Vanilla dough

  5.3 oz (150 g) unsalted butter, room temperature
  3.5 oz (100 g) confectioners' sugar
  1/2 tsp (2 g) salt
  1.9 oz (55 g) white almond flour; see p. 86
  2.1 oz (60 g) egg yolk (about 3 yolks)
  8.8 oz (250 g) all-purpose flour
  1 tsp (5 g) vanilla sugar

Chocolate dough

  5.3 oz (150 g) unsalted butter, room temperature
  3.5 oz (100 g) confectioners' sugar
  1/2 tsp (2 g) salt
  1.2 oz (35 g) white almond flour; see p. 86
  2.1 oz (60 g) egg yolk (about 3 yolks)
  0.9 oz (25 g) cocoa powder, preferably Valrhona
  8.4 (240 g) all-purpose flour

  1 beaten egg for glazing

1. Make both kinds of dough, using butter, confectioners' sugar, salt, almond flour and egg yolks.
2. Add flour and vanilla sugar to make vanilla dough.
3. Add sieved chocolate powder and flour to make chocolate dough.
4. Roll out each piece of dough, 3/4 inch thick.
5. Refrigerate for 30 minutes.
6. Whisk the egg and use it to brush both pieces of dough, placing one on top of the other.
7. Leave in the freezer for 30 minutes.
8. Using a large sharp knife, cut into 3/4 inch wide strips.
9. Separate the strips. Using the beaten egg as glue, join the strips into small "chessboard" lengths. Place in the freezer for 1 hour.
10. Preheat oven to 350°F.
11. Using a sharp knife, cut into 8 mm wide cookies, 0.4 oz (11 g) each.
12. Place on a baking sheet covered with parchment paper and bake for 10–12 minutes.

Chevy Raisin Brownies makes about 50

•

Finely chopped Californian raisins make these scrumptious brownies extra chewy. See photo, p. 90.

   5.3 oz (150 g) roasted hazelnuts
   2.5 oz (70 g) unsalted butter, room temperature
   4 oz (115 g) bittersweet chocolate (Valrhona Extra Amèr 67% or Marabou dark)
   3.5 oz (100 g) finely chopped raisins
   1.8 oz (50 g) sugar
   3.5 oz (100 g) brown sugar
   3.5 oz (100 g) egg (about 2 eggs)
   1.1 oz (30 g) quick-cooking oats
   3.5 oz (100 g) special flour (extra protein)
   1/2 tsp (3 g) baking powder
   1/2 tsp (2 g) salt

1. Preheat oven to 400°F. Place the hazelnuts on a baking sheet and roast for about 10 minutes until golden brown.
2. Rub the nuts, using a tea towel, to remove the skins.
3. Wrapping the nuts in the tea towel, smash them into large pieces with a heavy saucepan.
4. Boil the butter in a microwave oven or saucepan.
5. Finely chop the chocolate and stir into the butter until melted.
6. Finely chop the raisins into a sticky paste and add to the chocolate mixture.
7. Add all the ingredients, apart from the nuts, and mix to a smooth batter
8. Preheat oven to 425°F.
9. Fill small, round, greased muffin pans with the batter, or make mounds directly on parchment paper. Bake for 5 minutes, removing while still soft. Leave to cool.
10. Temper 2.5 oz (70 g) bittersweet chocolate; see p. 35. Using a paper cone with a small hole cut in one end, pipe out stripes of chocolate to decorate the brownies.

Strassburger makes about 60

• •

The Strassburger is one of the classic cookies, which should be very fragile and have a slightly sandy consistency. I have chosen chocolate with a well-rounded flavor, Valrhona Grand Cru Pur Caraïbe 66.5%, for coating the pointed end of the cookie. See photo, p. 90.

   6.3 oz (180 g) unsalted butter, room temperature
   2.5 oz (70 g) confectioners' sugar
   1 tsp (6 g) vanilla sugar
   2.1 oz (60 g) egg yolk (about 3 yolks)
   6.8 oz (195 g) all-purpose flour
   1.1 oz (30 g) cocoa powder, preferably Valrhona
   1/2 tsp (2 g) salt
   about 3.5 oz (100 g) raspberry jam of the highest quality

For coating
   7 oz (200 g) bittersweet chocolate (Valrhona Grand Cru Pur Caraïbe 66.5% or Marabou dark)

1. Cream together the butter, sugar and salt.
2. Mix in the egg yolks by hand, or use a hand blender.
3. Sift together the flour and cocoa. Add to the egg-mixture and whisk thoroughly.
4. Preheat oven to 400°F.
5. Using a pastry bag with a fluted no. 8 tip, pipe the mixture into small shell-shapes, pointed at one end.
6. Bake for about 8 minutes until nicely brown. Leave to cool.
7. Spread raspberry jam on the flat underside and sandwich two shells.
8. Temper the chocolate; see p. 35. Coat the pointed end of the cookie. Place on parchment paper and leave to harden.

Raspberry jam for baking
   35 oz (1000 g) raspberries
   26.5 oz (750 g) sugar
   juice of 2 lemons

1. Mix the ingredients in a 4-quart stainless steel saucepan. Cover with plastic wrap and leave to marinate for 24 hours.
2. Place the saucepan on the stove and bring to a boil, stirring continuously. Skim off the surface. Boil to 215–225°F and pour into hot, sterilized glass jars. Fill right to the top and seal immediately. Turn the glass jar upside down.

I only add 17.5 oz (500 g) sugar when making jam for use in desserts, and for waffles, pancakes, etc. When baking, however, I want a thicker jam and add 26.5 oz (750 g) sugar per 35 oz (1000 g) berries. Sealing the jars immediately and turning them upside down will form a vacuum, which ensures that the jam can be kept for a long time. Store in a refrigerator.

Chocolate Cookies.

Top row: New York, New York Brownies, p. 87, Chocolate
Diamond, p. 82 and Strassburger, p. 89.
Middle row: Chocolate Chip Cookie, p. 88, Chocolate Dream,
p. 91 and another Strassburger.
Bottom row: Brussels Cookie, p. 88, Chevy Raisin Brownie, p. 89
and Chocolate Shortbread p. 91.

Chocolate Dreams makes about 50

●

See photo, p. 90.

  6.3 oz (180 g) unsalted butter, room temperature
  6.3 oz (180 g) sugar
  7.4 oz (210 g) all-purpose flour
  0.9 oz (25 g) cocoa powder, preferably Valrhona
  1 tsp (5 g) hartshorn salt
  1/2 tsp (2 g) salt
  1 tsp (5 g) vanilla sugar

1. Cream together the sugar and butter.
2. Sift all the other ingredients together and add to the butter-mixture. Work into smooth dough.
3. Divide the dough into two, and roll out each piece into 1 inch diameter lengths.
4. Preheat oven to 300°F.
5. Cut the lengths into 0.4 oz (11 g) pieces (use letter scales for weighing).
6. Form into round balls and place on a baking sheet, covered with parchment paper.
7. Bake for 20–25 minutes until they feel light and are nicely browned.

Tip

Your "dreams" will deflate if you take them out too soon, or have the oven too hot.

Chocolate Shortbread makes about 50

●

See photo, p. 90.

Shortbread is a Scottish specialty that has a luscious, melting consistency. "Short" comes from the fact that the dough should be worked for as short a time as possible.

  8.8 oz (250 g) unsalted butter, room temperature
  4.4 oz (125 g) confectioners' sugar
  1/2 tsp (2 g) salt
  1.4 oz (40 g) egg yolk (about 2 yolks)
  7.9 oz (225 g) all-purpose flour
  0.9 oz (25 g) cocoa powder
  0.9 oz (25 g) crème fraîche 40%

  1 egg for glazing

1. Cream together the butter, sugar and salt.
2. Mix in the egg yolks.
3. Sift together the flour and cocoa and add to the egg-mixture. Using your hands, quickly work into dough.
4. Leave the dough in the refrigerator for at least 1 hour.
5. Preheat oven to 350°F.
6. Roll out the dough, 1 1/2 inch thick.
7. Brush the upper side with the beaten egg.
8. Using a fork, make a grid-work pattern in the dough.
9. Cut into 1 1/2 x 1 1/2 inch squares.
10. Place the squares on a baking sheet covered in parchment paper. Bake for 6–8 minutes until nicely brown.

Chocolate Petits Fours

These scrumptious tidbits make the perfect ending for a good meal, preferably with a strong espresso! Petits fours should not be too big; 0.4–0.5 oz (10–15 g) is about right.

Chocolate Luxemburgli makes about 40

• •

A Luxemburgli should be shiny on the outside and soft in the middle. The chocolate I have chosen here is Extra Amèr, which contains 67.5% cocoa from both forastero and criollo beans. This chocolate has a lasting, bitter taste.

Pâtisserie ganache
      4.4 oz (125 g) bittersweet chocolate (Valrhona Extra Amèr
            67% or Marabou dark)
      4.4 oz (125 g) heavy cream (1 3/4 cups)
      0.9 oz (25 g) honey

      9 oz (260 g) confectioners' sugar
      5.3 oz (150 g) almond flour; see p. 86
      0.7 oz (20 g) cocoa powder
      0.4 oz (10 g) apricot jelly
      1.1 oz (30 g) egg white (1 white)
      0.4 oz (10 g) water (2 tsp)

      3.2 oz (90 g) egg white (3 whites)
      1.8 oz (50 g) sugar
      lemon juice

DAY 1
Make the ganache for filling
1. Finely chop the chocolate and put in a plastic bowl.
2. Boil up the cream and honey and pour over the chocolate.
3. Using a plastic spoon, mix into a smooth and pliable ganache. Cover with plastic wrap and leave overnight.

DAY 2
4. Sift together confectioners' sugar, almond flour and cocoa.
5. Transfer to a bowl, add the apricot jelly and 1.1 oz (30 g) egg white. Using your hands, work into a smooth batter before adding the water.
6. Whisk 3.2 oz (90 g) egg white, lemon juice and sugar with an electric mixer on medium speed (or by hand) until stiff.
7. Mix half of the egg white mixture into the batter and work until completely smooth. Carefully fold in the remaining egg white.
8. Pour the batter into a pastry bag, with a smooth no. 8 tip.

9. Pipe out small balls onto parchment paper. Leave to dry for at least 30 minutes, or preferably overnight.
10. Preheat oven to 425°F.
11. Bake for 6–8 minutes using 2 baking sheets under the parchment paper to prevent the underside becoming too brown. Leave to cool.
12. If the cookies stick to the parchment, turn the paper over and brush with cold water. Leave for 5 minutes and the macaroons will loosen.
13. Using a pastry bag with a smooth no. 8 tip, pipe a hazelnut-sized ball of ganache on half the cookies. Sandwich with the remaining cookies.

Storage
If you don't eat them all up at one go, you can put them in an airtight plastic container and store in the freezer. They keep for several weeks, defrost quickly and taste wonderful.

Chocolate Tuiles makes about 40

•

See photo, p. 94.

      1.1 oz (30 g) hazelnuts
      1.4 oz (40 g) unsalted butter, room temperature
      3.5 oz (100 g) confectioners' sugar
      1.1 oz (30 g) water (2 tbs)
      1.1 oz (30 g) all-purpose flour
      0.5 oz (15 g) cocoa powder, preferably Valrhona

1. Preheat oven to 400°F.
2. Spread the hazelnuts on a baking sheet and roast for about 10 minutes until golden brown. Note that the nuts can easily burn when there are so few of them.
3. Rub the nuts in a tea towel to remove the skins. Chop finely and put aside.
4. Melt the butter and add water. Whisk in the flour, confectioners' sugar and cocoa powder to a smooth batter.
5. Leave the batter to swell for 1 hour.
6. Preheat oven to 350°F.
7. Brush out small 2 inch circles of batter onto parchment paper.
8. Sprinkle the circles with chopped nuts. Bake for 8 minutes until golden brown.
9. Immediately place the circles, while still soft, on a rolling pin. This will give them their characteristic curved shape when cooled.

Petits Fours. Top row: Chocolate Tartelette with raspberry, p. 95, Chestnut dipped in chocolate, p. 97, Chocolate Tartelette with lemon ganache and cherry, p. 96.
Middle: Pistachio Macaroon Sandwiches, p. 98.
Front row: Small Florentine, p. 95, small Sarah Bernhardt, p. 100, Chocolate Luxemburgli.

Petits Fours. Clockwise from the top: Chocolate Tuile, p. 92,
Florentine, p. 95, Amaretti, p. 96 and Chocolate Macaroon, p. 98.

Florentines makes about 30

• •

I have chosen Valrhona Grand Cru Guanaja, with cocoa beans from South America, for these florentines. This chocolate has an intense, bitter taste, which is well suited to this sweet cookie. This classic cookie should always be found on a tray of petits fours. See photos p. 93 and 94.

3.5 oz (100 g) almonds
2.6 oz (75 g) preserved orange peel
1.4 oz (40 g) sugar
1.4 oz (40 g) honey
2.6 oz (75 g) heavy cream (1/3 cup)
0.7 oz (20 g) unsalted butter
7 oz (200 g) bittersweet chocolate (Valrhona Grand Cru Guanaja 70.5% or Marabou dark)

1. Blanch the almonds.
2. Cut into fine strips and leave to dry on a tea towel.
3. Drain the orange peel on a rack before chopping finely.
4. Mix sugar, honey, cream and butter in a saucepan. Bring to a boil, stirring continuously. The batter is ready when it has reached 237°F and begins to come away from the edges.
5. Add the almonds and orange peel and mix thoroughly.
6. Preheat oven to 350°F.
7. Drop spoonfuls of the batter onto a baking sheet covered with parchment paper.
8. Moisten your palm with cold water and carefully flatten them.
9. Bake for 10–12 minutes until golden brown. You can use a cookie cutter to make perfect circles, alternatively you can bake the florentines in 1 1/4 inches round, greased muffin pans.
10. Leave to cool.
11. Temper the chocolate; see p. 35.
12. Brush the underside of the circles with chocolate and allow to harden. Repeat and use a fork to make a striped pattern in the chocolate.

Chocolate Tartelette with Raspberry
makes about 30

•

See photo, p. 93.

Sablé dough, using almond flour

2.6 oz (75 g) unsalted butter, room temperature
4.4 oz (125 g) all-purpose flour
1.8 oz (50 g) confectioners' sugar
0.5 oz (15 g) white almond flour; see p. 86
0.7 oz (20 g) egg yolk (1 yolk)
1 pinch (1 g) salt
1/2 tsp (2 g) vanilla sugar

Ganache

4.4 oz (125 g) heavy cream
0.9 oz (25 g) honey
4.4 oz (125 g) bittersweet chocolate (Valrhona Grand Cru Manjari 64.5% or Marabou dark)
0.9 oz (25 g) unsalted butter, room temperature
0.4 oz (10 g) cocoa powder for powdering
7 oz (200 g) raspberries
1 pot fresh peppermint

1. Mix the butter into 1/3 of the flour, using your fingers or a food processor.
2. Mix the rest of the ingredients into dough. Never overwork short crust pastry.
3. Cover in plastic wrap and leave for at least 1 hour, or overnight, in the refrigerator
4. Roll out the dough, 1/4 inch thick. Laying the dough over the rolling pin, roll out over a so-called petits fours pan.
5. Lightly powder with flour, and press the dough down into the indentations.
6. Prick the dough into place with a fork, and place out the petits fours pans on a baking sheet.
7. Place the baking sheet in the freezer for 30 minutes.
8. Preheat oven to 350°F.
9. Bake for 8–10 minutes until golden brown.
10. Leave to cool and unpan the pastry shells.

Ganache

11. Finely chop the chocolate and place in a plastic bowl.
12. Boil up the cream and honey and pour into the bowl.
13. Stir with a plastic spoon or hand blender, and mix into a smooth, pliable ganache. Add the butter and stir until melted.
14. Pour the ganache into the pastry shells, and leave to stiffen at room temperature.
15 Sift a little cocoa powder over the tartelettes, using a tea strainer.
16. Decorate with a raspberry and peppermint leaf.

Amaretti makes about 30

• •

This tasty almond cookie is a specialty from the Italian region of Switzerland. When I worked at the Confiserie Honold in Zürich, we filled the cookies using ganache flavored with Kirschwasser. You can use rum instead if you prefer. See photo, p. 94.

3.5 oz (100 g) almonds
0.9 oz (25 g) bitter almonds
4.4 oz (125 g) sugar
2.1 oz (60 g) egg white (2 whites)
8.8 oz (250 g) confectioners' sugar
2.1 oz (60 g) egg white (2 whites)
0.9 oz (25 g) confectioners' sugar for powdering

Kirsch sugar syrup
1.2 oz (35 g) confectioners' sugar
1.8 oz (50 g) Kirschwasser (about 1/4 cup)

Kirsch butter truffle
3.5 oz (100 g) bittersweet chocolate (Valrhona Grand Cru
   Guanaja 70.5% or Marabou dark)
0.9 oz (25 g) unsalted butter
0.5 oz (15 g) confectioners' sugar
1.8 oz (50 g) Kirschwasser (about 1/4 cup)

DAY 1
1. Blanch the almonds and dry in a tea towel.
2. Mix the almonds and sugar for a couple of minutes, in a food processor or blender.
3. Add 2.1 oz (60 g) egg white and mix to a paste.
4. Transfer the paste to a bowl. By hand or using an electric mixer, work in the rest of the egg white and confectioners' sugar, a little at the time, to a smooth paste.
5. Using a pastry bag with a smooth no. 8 tip, pipe out small crests of paste. Leave to dry overnight at room temperature.

DAY 2
6. Powder with a thin layer of confectioners' sugar. Squeeze the crests gently.
7. Preheat oven to 425°F.
8. Bake for about 5 minutes, using double baking sheets to prevent the bottom of the cookies becoming too brown. Leave to cool.
9. Place in the freezer for about 1 hour.
10. If they stick to the parchment, turn the paper over and brush with cold water. Leave for 5 minutes and the macaroons will loosen.
11. Make the sugar syrup: Whisk together the confectioners' sugar and the Kirschwasser. Brush the underside of the cookies.

12. Make the truffle: Melt the finely chopped chocolate in a microwave oven, stirring regularly, and bring to 131°F. Firstly add the cold butter, stir until melted and finally add the sugar and Kirschwasser. Leave at room temperature to stiffen for 30 minutes.
13. Fill a paper cone with the truffle. Cut a hole in the cone and pipe a small knob on the underside of half the cookies.
14. Sandwich two cookies together with the truffle.

Storage
These can be kept frozen for several weeks in an airtight container.

Chocolate Tartelette with Lemon Ganache and Cherries makes about 30

•

See photo, p. 94.

1 batch Sablé dough with almond flour; see p. 86

Lemon ganache
3.5 oz (100 g) bittersweet chocolate (Valrhona Grand Cru
   Manjari 64.5% or Marabou dark)
1.4 oz (40 g) lemon juice (about 3 tbs)
1.4 oz (40 g) sugar
1.4 oz (40 g) unsalted butter
1.4 oz (40 g) egg yolk (about 2 yolks)

3.5 oz (100 g) fresh cherries
0.7 oz (20 g) confectioners' sugar for powdering

1. Using the Sablé dough, make the tartelette shells as in the recipe on p. 95, following steps 1–10.

Lemon ganache
2. Finely chop the chocolate and put in a plastic bowl.
3. Mix the lemon juice, sugar, butter and egg yolk in a small saucepan.
4. Simmer, stirring continuously, until the mixture begins to thicken.
5. Continue to whisk the mixture thoroughly after you have removed it from the heat to prevent the egg yolk coagulating.
6. Pass the mixture through a strainer into the bowl of chopped chocolate. Using a plastic spoon or hand blender, mix to a smooth and pliable ganache.
7. Scrape the ganache into the tartelette shells, and leave to stiffen at room temperature.
8. Powder with confectioners' sugar through a tea strainer. Decorate with a cherry.

Chestnuts makes about 35

● ●

This classic French petits fours is just as eye-catching as it is delicious. Just remember that the chocolate caramel should not be too cool when you dip the chestnuts. See photo, p. 94.

7 oz (200 g) bittersweet chocolate (Valrhona Grand Cru Pur Caraïbe 66.5% or Marabou dark)

7 oz (200 g) crème de marrons, preserved (or see Chestnut Mousse, p. 144)

0.4 oz (10 g) dark rum (2 tsp)

0.9 oz (25 g) confectioners' sugar, for rolling and shaping the paste

Chocolate caramel
17.5 oz (500 g) sugar
7 oz (200 g) water (3 cups)
0.9 oz (25 g) cocoa powder
5.3 oz (150 g) glucose

1. Finely shop the chocolate and melt in a microwave oven. Take out the bowl and stir occasionally.
2. At 131°F, add the chestnut cream and rum. Mix to a paste.
3. Leave to cool in a refrigerator for 1 hour.
4. Powder the table with confectioners' sugar, and roll the paste into a rod.
5. Cut into 0.4 oz (10–12 g) pieces. Roll into balls, using the confectioners' sugar.
6. Point the balls at one end, to resemble chestnuts.
7. Leave in the freezer to stiffen.

Making the chocolate caramel
8. Mix sugar, water and cocoa powder in a 1-quart saucepan. Boil up and skim with a spoon.
9. Add glucose and boil to 313°F. Use a thermometer or do a finger test; see p. 44. Remove the saucepan from the heat.
10. Stick a fork in the bottom of the chestnut and dip into the caramel. Let the caramel run into a long thin tip. Cut off the tip at 1/2–1 inch.

Dipping the frozen chestnut in chocolate caramel.

Important! *Keep the saucepan at a low heat while dipping. Never stir the caramel, once made, or the sugar will crystallize, making it impossible to work with.*

Chocolate Macaroons

makes about 40

• •

Macaroons, "macarons de Nancy," originate in France. They always contain two parts almond and one part sugar to achieve their cracked surface. I have made the butter cream using egg white rather than egg yolk. In this way the butter cream has a firmer consistency and its flavor interplays better with the chocolate. A powerful chocolate is required, such as Valrhona Grand Cru Guanaja 70.5%. See photo, p. 94.

Macaroon paste

4.4 oz (125 g) almonds, preferably Spanish
4.4 oz (125 g) sugar
4.4 oz (125 g) sugar
2.1 oz (60 g) egg white (about 2 whites)

Chocolate butter-cream

3.2 oz (90 g) egg white (about 3 whites)
1 tsp freshly squeezed lemon juice
4.4 oz (125 g) sugar
8.8 oz (250 g) unsalted butter, room temperature
3.5 oz (100 g) bittersweet chocolate (Valrhona Grand Cru Guanaja 70.5% or marabou dark)

For coating

17.5 oz (500 g) semisweet chocolate (Valrhona Caraque 56% or Marabou dark)

1. Blanch the almonds and dry in a tea towel.
2. Put the almonds and 4.4 oz (125 g) sugar in a blender or food processor. Mix for about a minute into almond paste.
3. Scrape the paste into a bowl and add the remaining sugar (4.4 oz) and 1/3 of the egg white. Mix until smooth.
4. Work the rest of the egg white, half at a time, into the paste.
5. Preheat oven to 350°F.
6. Using a pastry bag with a no. 8 tip, pipe out 1 inch coins of paste onto a parchment-covered baking sheet.
7. Bake for 10–12 minutes, until golden brown.
8. If they stick to the parchment, turn the paper over and brush with cold water. Leave for 5 minutes and the macaroons will loosen.

Chocolate butter-cream

9. Whisk the egg yolk, lemon juice and sugar in a metal bowl. Place the bowl in boiling water and whisk with an electric mixer.
10. Remove bowl from the water when the mixture has reached 143°F. Continue to whisk at medium speed until the batter has cooled.
11. Add the butter and whisk at low speed for 5–10 minutes until porous.

12. Finely chop the chocolate and melt in a microwave oven, stirring occasionally. Bring to 122°F.
13. Pour the chocolate slowly and evenly into the butter-cream and mix thoroughly.
14. Using a pastry bag with a no. 8 tip, and pipe a small ball of butter-cream onto each macaroon.
15. Leave to cool for 30 minutes in a refrigerator.
16. Take out the macaroons and leave in room temperature for 10 minutes before dipping. (If they are too cold when dipped, the chocolate coating will become lusterless and moist.)

Coating

18. Temper the chocolate; see p. 35. Dip the macaroons with the butter cream downwards. Remove excess chocolate by scraping on the edge of the bowl. Place on parchment paper and leave to harden.

Pistachio Macaroon Sandwiches

• •

See photo, p. 93.

Macaroon paste

2.3 oz (65 g) pistachios
2.3 oz (65 g) sugar
4.4 oz (125 g) sugar
4.4 oz (125 g) confectioners' sugar
2.1 oz (60 g) egg white (about 2 whites)

Patisserie ganache

See recipe for Sarah Bernhardt, p. 100

For coating

See recipe for Chocolate Macaroons, above

Follow steps 1–9 in the chocolate macaroon recipe.

1. Make the patisserie ganache; see p. 100.
2. Sandwich the macaroons together with ganache.
3. Temper the chocolate.
4. Dip the macaroon sandwiches halfway into the chocolate. Place on parchment paper to harden.

Useful tip

By using granulated sugar in the macaroons, a beautiful cracked surface is achieved.

Note

For the most esthetic results when dipping, you need to make a generous amount of melted chocolate. Any excess chocolate can be left to harden and re-used.

Storage

Macaroons will keep for about a week if stored cool in an airtight container. Do not keep in a refrigerator or they will become moist.

Sarah Bernhardt   makes about 40

• •

This classic confection was created in the early 1900s to celebrate the famous French actress, and can now be found over the whole world. There are slightly different ways of making them, but ganache is usually used as a filling. I flavor the ganache with French orange liqueur, preferably Grand Marnier Rouge or Cointreau.

1 batch macaroon paste; see p. 98

Grand Marnier pâtisserie ganache
3.5 oz (100 g) lightly salted almonds, not blanched
8.8 oz (250 g) bittersweet chocolate (Valrhona Grand Cru
    Manjari 64.5% or Marabou dark)
8.8 oz (250 g) heavy cream (about 1 cup)
1.8 oz (50 g) orange-flower honey
0.9 oz (25 g) unsalted butter
0.9 oz (25 g) Grand Marnier Rouge (1/8 cup)

For coating
10.5 oz (300 g) semisweet chocolate (Valrhona Caraque
    56% or Marabou dark)
roasted almonds for decoration

DAY 1
1. Make the macaroon bases; see p. 98, following steps 1–9, and freeze.

Grand Marnier ganache
2. Finely chop the chocolate and place in a bowl.
3. Boil together the cream, honey and butter and pour the mixture over the chocolate.
4. Using a plastic spoon, mix to a smooth and pliable ganache. Cover with plastic film and leave at room temperature to stiffen.

DAY 2
5. Remove the macaroons from the freezer and cover with ganache, using a small knife or spoon. Leave to stiffen in the refrigerator for 30 minutes. Remove and bring to room temperature before dipping.

Coating
6. Temper the chocolate and dip the macaroons, following the recipe for Chocolate Macaroons on p. 98.

Decorate with a lightly roasted almond, or a flake of gold leaf if you're feeling extravagant.

Boiled Chocolate Meringue makes about 20

• •

4.4 oz (125 g) water (2/3 cup)
8.8 oz (250 g) sugar
3.5 oz (100 g) egg white (about 3 whites)
1 tsp freshly squeezed lemon juice
0.9 oz (25 g) sugar
5.3 oz (150 g) bittersweet chocolate (Valrhona Grand Cru
  Guanaja 70.5% or Marabou dark)
1.4 oz (40 g) lukewarm water (1/8 cup)

1. Measure the water into a 1-quart saucepan. Add the sugar
   and whisk until fully dissolved. Boil up and skim.
2. Using a brush dipped in cold water, wash down the inside of
   the saucepan. Heat the sugar syrup to 110°C
3. Whisk the egg white, lemon juice and 0.9 oz (25 g) sugar until
   stiff.

4. Vigorously boil the sugar syrup to 252°F (use a thermometer
   or do a finger test; see p. 44).
5. Stirring continuously, pour the sugar syrup into the egg white
   mixture. Whisk at low speed for about 10 minutes until the
   batter has cooled.
6. Finely chop the chocolate and melt in a microwave oven or
   double-boiler until 131°F.
7. Stir the chocolate with a baking spatula. Add the lukewarm
   water and stir to a smooth cream.
8. Add the chocolate cream to the batter and stir until porous.
9. Using a pastry bag with a fluted no. 12 tip, pipe s-shaped
   meringues onto parchment paper. Leave to dry for at least
   3 hours or overnight.
10. Preheat oven to 300°F. Bake for about 10 minutes, turn off the
    heat and leave for a further 30 minutes.

The real finesse with these meringues is that they are somewhat
soft in the middle. To keep them fresh, store in the freezer. Take
them out about 10 minutes before serving.

petits pains au chocolat, brioches, and other goodies

These wonderful classic French pastries, particularly the chocolate varieties with a bittersweet filling such as Valrhona Grand Cru Guanaja, are best enjoyed with a cup of strong coffee.

There are different versions of the story as to how the croissant was born. One version has it that when the Turks stormed Budapest in 1686, they tried to dig a tunnel under the walls to invade the town. Some night-working bakers discovered the attempt, raised the alarm and saved the town. In celebration, the bakers created a pastry in the shape of a crescent, the symbol of the Ottoman Empire.

A similar story is told of the siege of Vienna in 1683. Well, I'm not sure which version is true, but one thing I do know is that the croissant came to Paris from Vienna. But not until 1920, when a Parisian pastry chef began to roll butter into his dough. It was a great success; people came from all over Paris to his patisserie to buy these delicious pastries.

Do not work the dough for too long or this will develop gluten, making the dough viscous. The resulting pastry will be leathery instead of crispy.

Clockwise: Chocolate Rolls, p. 106, Croissant, p. 106 and 108,
Chocolate Coil, p. 108 and Chocolate Pistache Craquelin, p. 110.

Petits Pains au Chocolat   makes 16

• •

See photo, p. 102.

0.7 oz (20 g) yeast
4.4 oz (125 g) water (2/3 cup)
5.3 oz (150 g) milk (3/4 cup)
17.5 oz (500 g) fortified flour
1.9 oz (55 g) sugar
0.4 oz (10 g) salt
10.5 oz (300 g) unsalted butter
7 oz (200 g) bittersweet chocolate (Valrhona Grand Cru
    Guanaja 70.5% or Marabou dark)
2 eggs for glazing

DAY 1

1. In a 2-quart bowl, dissolve the yeast in the water, then whisk
   in the milk.
2. Pour the flour, sugar and salt into the bowl. Work the dough
   by hand for about 5 minutes, or 3 minutes in a food processor,
   until it comes away from the sides of the bowl.
3. Cover with a cloth and leave to rise for 2 hours at room
   temperature.
4. Fold the dough over itself and press out the air. Cover with
   plastic wrap and leave in the refrigerator overnight (at least
   8–12 hours). Check after 1 hour. Depending on the temperature in the refrigerator, the dough may have begun to rise
   again. If so, punch down the dough again to prevent so-called
   wild fermentation.

DAY 2

5. Cut a cross over the top of the dough. Roll out each section on
   a floured surface, turning the dough through 90 degrees with
   each rolling.
6. Beat the cold butter with the rolling pin to soften it, and place
   in the middle of the dough. Fold over the four corners of the
   dough, making sure that the butter is completely encased.
   Seal the edges.
7. Lightly flour the dough and work surface. Roll the dough into
   a rectangle, 16 x 28 inches (use a ruler). Roll outwards from
   the middle of the dough. Brush off excess flour.
8. Fold the dough into thirds. Wrap with plastic and return to
   the refrigerator for 30 minutes. Repeat this procedure twice to
   ensure that the butter is distributed evenly throughout. Finally
   allow the dough to rest for 30 minutes so that the layers of
   the pastry will not be destroyed.
9. Roll out the dough to a 16 x 28 inch rectangle.
10. Trim the edges with a knife and ruler and cut the dough into
    2 lengths of similar width.
11. Divide each length into 8 equal pieces.
12. Ensuring the chocolate is at room temperature, cut it into
    16 pieces.

13. Beat the egg and glaze the oblongs of dough. Put a piece of
    chocolate in each and fold the dough into a triangle. Place
    8 triangles on each baking sheet.
14. Glaze with egg, and leave to rise in a warm place for about
    2 hours, until they have doubled in size.
15. Preheat oven to 400°F. Glaze the dough a final time with the
    egg and bake for 12–15 minutes until golden brown. Take out
    and cool immediately on a rack.

Important!

Do not skip any of the steps if you want your puff pastry to be the best possible.

Croissants

If you wish to bake ordinary croissants, cut the dough into 16
triangles and roll them up, folding the ends in over the middle.
Lightly glaze the croissants with beaten egg.

Chocolate Rolls   makes about 25

• •

**This is Sweden's favorite Danish pastry. In Denmark, they
always weigh the dough and roll in 50% butter to make
their superb pastries. Visit Kransekagehuset, just off
Strøget, the next time you're in Copenhagen. Try their
fantastic Danish pastries and don't forget to taste their
homemade jam. See photo, p. 105.**

1 batch vanilla cream, see Othello p. 132.

Chocolate icing

7 oz (200 g) sugar
3.5 oz (100 g) water (1/2 cup)
1.8 oz (50 g) glucose

2.6 oz (75 g) bittersweet chocolate (Valrhona Grand Cru
    70.5% or Marabou dark)

Follow the instructions for Fondant, p. 74.

Danish puff pastry

- 21 oz (600 g) fortified flour
- 8.8 oz (250 g) water (1 cup)
- 1.8 oz (50 g) yeast
- 3.5 oz (100 g) egg (about 2 eggs)
- 1.4 oz (40 g) egg yolk (about 2 yolks)
- 1.2 oz (35 g) sugar
- 0.4 oz (10 g) salt
- 22 oz (625 g) unsalted butter
- 2 eggs for glazing

1. Boil the vanilla cream and leave to cool.
2. Prepare the chocolate glaze (see Peppermint Pastilles, preparation of Fondant, p. 74).
3. Place the flour in the freezer for 1 hour before making the dough.
4. Pour the water into a 2-quart bowl and dissolve the yeast with a whisk. Add the other ingredients and work by hand until the dough comes away from the edge of the bowl (or run 2–3 minutes in a food processor).
5. Wrap well in plastic and freeze for 15 minutes.
6. Place the dough on a floured surface and roll it into a 14 x 8 inch rectangle. Using the rolling pin, hit the butter a few times so that it softens but is still cold.
7. Fold the edges over the butter to completely encase it. Wrap in plastic and place in refrigerator for 30 minutes to bring the butter and the dough to the same temperature.

8. Lightly flour the work surface and carefully roll out the dough, working from the inside, into an 18 x 30 inch rectangle. Fold the dough in thirds. This is the first "turn." Rotate the dough through 90 degrees and carefully roll out the dough again, working from the inside, into an 18 x 30 inch rectangle. Fold the dough in thirds. This is the second turn.
9. Wrap in plastic and refrigerate for 30 minutes.
10. Roll out the dough again and repeat the process for the third turn. The dough is now ready for making Danish pastry.
11. Roll out the dough about 1/2 inch thick. Lightly flour the topside and underside. Trim the edges with a knife and cut out 3 1/2 inch squares.
12. Using a plastic pastry bag, pipe out 0.7 oz (20 g) balls of the cold vanilla cream, on each square. Fold the corners over the cream and turn the squares over. Place them in two parchment-covered baking sheets.
13. Glaze with beaten egg and leave to rise for 45 minutes.
14. Preheat oven to 425°F. Glaze again, and bake for about 15 minutes until golden brown.
15. Finely chop the chocolate and melt in a microwave oven or double boiler. Warm the fondant to 95°F in a double boiler or bowl placed in boiling water. Using a baking spatula, mix the chocolate into smooth glaze.
16. Decorate the cold Danish pastries with a tablespoon of glaze.

Vanilla cream is piped onto the squares of Danish pastry.

These are then folded and turned over.

Chocolate croissants or coils

If you want to make chocolate croissants, follow the recipe for chocolate rolls, but divide the rolled out dough length-wise and use a sharp knife to cut out 12 triangles. Fill them with the chocolate filling described below. Use 1 teaspoon for each and roll them into croissants (see croissants, p. 106). Leave to rise on parchment paper.

If you want to make chocolate coils, divide the dough as for croissants and brush the chocolate filling on each length, using a spatula. Roll up the lengths. Placing the join downwards, cut each length into 14 coils. Place them on 2 baking sheets covered with parchment paper. Fold the edges under the coils so they do not unroll during baking. See photo, p. 105.

Chocolate filling

    1.8 oz (50 g) almonds
    1.8 oz (50 g) walnuts
    0.9 oz (25 g) preserved orange peel
    5.3 oz (150 g) brown sugar
    0.9 oz (25 g) cocoa
    0.5 oz (15 g) cornstarch
    1.8 oz (50 g) unsalted butter, room temperature

In a blender or food processor, pulverize the almonds and walnuts. Then add orange peel, brown sugar, cocoa and maizena and work to a flour. Add the butter and mix to a smooth paste.

Tip

Drink a cup of hot chocolate, or maybe even a glass of Gammel Dansk, with these delicacies and you'll find yourself transported to Copenhagen!

Storage

Dough for pains au chocolat, croissants and Danish pastry can be frozen before it has risen, placed on a baking sheet. Do not freeze for more than a week, however. Take out and allow to rise for 90 minutes before baking.

You can also freeze the finished pastries, firstly on a baking sheet and then in plastic bags. Heat for about 5 minutes before serving.

Brioches   makes about 20

● ●

The name originates from the Brie district of France. Brioches should have a strong butter flavor, but without feeling fatty. The secret is to work the dough smooth and elastic for a long time before the butter (at room tempera-ture) is added. The French usually add 8–13 oz butter per lb flour, but their Brioches are nevertheless light and fluffy when we eat them.

Adding cocoa and finely chopped chocolate will give these Brioches an absolutely sensational flavor. I have found that Valrhona Grand Cru Pur Caraïbe or Valrhona Gran Couva are the best kinds for this recipe.

These Brioches makes an excellent starter, with a slice of duck or goose liver and a glass of top-quality Sauterne.

Brioche dough

    0.7 oz (20 g) yeast
    8.8 oz (250 g) egg (about 5 eggs)
    17.5 oz (500 g) fortified flour
    0.7 oz (20 g) salt
    2.1 oz (60 g) sugar
    13.1 oz (375 g) unsalted butter

For chocolate Brioche

    0.9 oz (25 g) cocoa powder, preferably Valrhona
    7 oz (200 g) bittersweet chocolate (Valrhona Grand Cru
        Pur Caraïbe 66.5% or Marabou dark)

    2 eggs for glazing

DAY 1

1. Place the yeast in a large bowl. Add the egg and whisk until the yeast is dissolved.
2. Add flour, salt and sugar. Work into viscous and elastic dough for about 10 minutes in a food processor, or about 20 minutes by hand. You should be able to stretch out the dough really thinly without it breaking.
3. Add the butter, a quarter at a time. Work the dough smooth and shiny each time.
4. Cover with a cloth and leave to rise for about 2 hours in a warm place, until the dough has doubled in size. Rework the dough one final time.
5. For the chocolate version: add both the cocoa and finely chopped chocolate when the dough has risen for 2 hours.
6. Cover with plastic wrap and place the dough in the refrig-erator overnight, 12–24 hours.

Divide dough with the side of your hand into 2 balls, one twice as large than the other.

DAY 2

7. Place the dough on a lightly floured work surface and fold it into a "parcel."
8. If you want to make small Brioches, grease 20 fluted individual tins with butter.
9. Roll 20 balls of dough and place on one side. Using the side of your hand, divide the balls into unequal portions (1/3 and 2/3). See photo above.
10. Place one large ball in each tin. Make an indentation in each ball and nestle the small ball in each indentation.
    (If you want to make a large Brioche, divide the dough into 4 parts and form into balls. Grease a large, fluted baking pan and place 3 of the balls in the bottom of the pan and the fourth on top. You can also make a large Brioche with 2 balls of plain dough and 2 balls of chocolate dough.)
11. Carefully glaze the Brioches with beaten egg. Be careful to prevent any egg running down the sides of the tins or the Brioches will stick, and not rise so well in the oven.
12. Leave to rise at room temperature for 1 hour, or 1/2 hour for the small Brioches, until they have doubled in size.
13. Preheat oven to 425°F. Lightly glaze the Brioches with egg. Make 6 cuts with a pair of scissors round the large Brioche, but not the small ones.
14. Bake the large Brioche for 45–50 minutes, or the small ones for 8–9 minutes, until nicely brown.
15. Immediately un-tin the Brioches and leave to cool on racks.

Chocolate and plain Brioche dough mixed.

Storage

First freeze on baking sheets and then in plastic bags. If you heat them at 400°F for 5 minutes before serving, they will almost seem freshly baked. The dough can be frozen in airtight containers for a week at most. The yeast continues to consume sugar from the dough and after 7 days will start to lose its ability to rise.

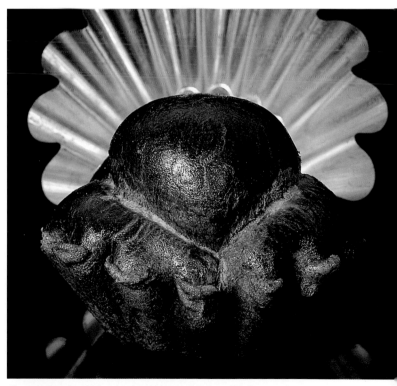

The Brioche should be un-tinned immediately and left to cool on racks.

Chocolate Mint Buns — makes 20

● ●

The peppermint gives extra zest to these buns and always goes well with chocolate. Try them hot with chocolate mousse.

1 batch Brioche dough, without chocolate, see p. 108

2 eggs for glazing
1 pot fresh peppermint
10.5 oz (300 g) bittersweet chocolate (Valrhona Grand Cru Pur Caraïbe 66.5% or Marabou dark)

DAY 1

Make a batch of Brioche dough without chocolate.

DAY 2

1. Finely chop the chocolate and most of the peppermint. Work into the chilled dough.
2. Divide the dough into 20 buns and place them on a parchment covered baking sheet. Glaze with the beaten egg. Press a peppermint leaf on top of each bun and leave to rise for about 1.5 hours at room temperature.
3. Preheat oven to 425°F, and bake the buns for 8–9 minutes, until golden brown.
4. Immediately place on racks to cool.

Pistachio Chocolate Craquelins — makes 12

● ●

These crispy cookies are a delicious combination of pistachio and chocolate. See photo, p. 105.

Quick puff pastry

Quick puff pastry
1.8 oz (50 g) pistachio nuts

8.8 oz (250 g) all-purpose flour
8.8 oz (250 g) unsalted butter
1 tsp (5 g) salt
3.5 oz (100 g) water (1/2 cup)
1 tsp freshly squeezed lemon juice
0.7 oz (20 g) egg yolk (about 1 yolk)
2.6 oz (75 g) bittersweet chocolate (Valrhona Grand Cru Guanaja 70.5% or Marabou dark)

all-purpose flour
granulated sugar
1 egg for glazing

Chocolate icing; see chocolate rolls, p. 106.

1. Mix the pistachio nuts to a paste in a blender or food processor.
2. Sift the flour onto the work surface. Cut the cold butter into small cubes.
3. Mix the butter, flour and salt until they resemble breadcrumbs.
4. Add the pistachio paste, water, lemon juice and egg yolk. Work the mixture into dough, leaving lumps of butter in the dough.
5. Wrap in plastic and leave for 30 minutes in a refrigerator.
6. Roll out 2 "turns," as for ordinary puff pastry. Refrigerate for 30 minutes.
7. Roll out 2 more turns and refrigerate for another 30 minutes.
8. Finely chop the chocolate.
9. Roll out the dough 1/4 inch thick. Brush the dough with beaten egg and sprinkle over with the chopped chocolate.
10. Roll up the dough tightly, and cut into 12 coils.
11. Dip one side of the coil in flour and place it on a bed of sugar. Roll out into cup sized discs and leave for 30 minutes, on a baking sheet covered with parchment paper.
12. Preheat oven to 425°F. Bake for 8–9 minutes until golden brown.
13. Leave to cool on racks.
14. Make chocolate icing, using the recipe on p. 106, and glaze the cookies.

Roll out the discs in sugar.

Grating chocolate over the rolled-out dough.

Chocolate Brioches, p. 108 and Chocolate Mint Buns, p. 110

Chocolate Jam

This chocolate jam tastes excellent on a fresh-baked Brioche or croissant.

1 vanilla pod
2 tins condensed milk (14 oz)
1.8 oz (50 g) cocoa powder, preferably Valrhona
2.6 oz (75 g) bittersweet chocolate (Valrhona Grand Cru
   Guanaja 70.5% or Marabou dark)
1 tsp (5 g) salt
2 tsp (10 g) balsamic vinegar
2.6 oz (75 g) orange-flower honey
8.8 oz (250 g) raw sugar

1. Divide the vanilla pod lengthwise and scrape the seeds into a saucepan.
2. Add the condensed milk, cocoa, finely chopped chocolate, salt, balsamic vinegar, honey and sugar.
3. Bring to a boil, stirring continuously, until the mixture is 220°F. If you have no thermometer, lift up the spoon—if a drop remains attached to it, the mixture is ready.
4. Rinse glass jars and sterilize in the oven at 200°F for 10 minutes.
5. Fill the jars with jam. Seal immediately and turn upside down to create a vacuum. Store in a refrigerator.

Chocolate jam on a piece of baguette.

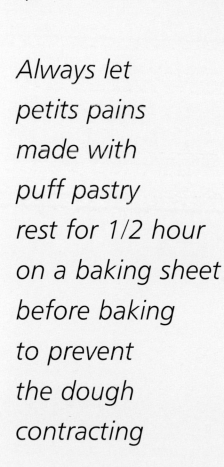

Tip

Always let petits pains made with puff pastry rest for 1/2 hour on a baking sheet before baking to prevent the dough contracting

CHAPTER 7

chocolate cakes

These cakes can be made well before serving. They are excellent for afternoon tea or can also be served with fruit salad or homemade ice cream.

Truffle Cake   about 12 slices

● ●

This Swiss specialty has a powerful chocolate taste and will keep fresh and moist for a whole week. Goes very well with a cup of strong coffee. I baked this cake for the first meeting of the Chocolate Academy in Malmö in the early 1980s.

1 loaf pan, about 12" long

butter and flour for lining the loaf pan

1.6 oz (45 g) hazelnuts
2.3 oz (65 g) almonds
2.3 oz (65 g) sugar
1.6 oz (45 g) all-purpose flour
1.6 oz (45 g) cocoa powder, preferably Valrhona
1 tsp (5 g) baking powder
1.6 oz (45 g) unsalted butter
4.9 oz (140 g) egg yolk (about 7 yolks)
6.3 oz (180 g) egg whites (about 5 whites)
2.3 oz (65 g) sugar
1 tsp freshly squeezed lemon juice

1 batch patisserie ganache, see Sarah Bernhardt, p. 100
    (omit Grand Marnier).

2.8 oz (80 g) bittersweet chocolate

DAY 1

1. Preheat oven to 400°F. Spread the hazelnuts on a baking sheet and roast for about 10 minutes until golden brown. Rub them in a tea towel to remove skins. Allow to cool, and grind finely.
2. Blanch the almonds. Pulverize in a food processor and mix with the sugar into a paste.
3. Sieve the flour, cocoa and baking powder and mix in the ground hazelnuts. Melt the butter.
4. Lower oven to 350°F.
5. Whisk the egg yolk and almond paste for 10 minutes.
6. Whisk the egg white, lemon juice and sugar until stiff.

7. Fold the egg-almond mixture into the egg white, together with the sieved ingredients and powdered nuts. Taking a spoonful, mix it carefully with the melted butter and pour back into the batter.
8. Pour the batter into the loaf pan, greased with butter and floured, ensuring that it comes a good way up the edges. Bake for 60–70 minutes. Use a cake tester to see if middle of the cake is baked.
9. Remove from the oven and leave for 5 minutes. Turn out onto a rack and leave to mature overnight in a refrigerator.
10. Make the patisserie ganache, see Sarah Bernhardt, p. 100. Omit Grand Marnier to keep the chocolate taste purer.

DAY 2

11. Carefully cut out a wedge shape from the center of the cake. See photo on opposite page.
12. Fill the hole in the cake with ganache. Replace the wedge with the sharp edge up. Spread ganache over the wedge as evenly as possible with a spatula, to resemble a roof. Leave to stiffen for 1 hour in the refrigerator.
13. Temper the chocolate; see p. 35. Dip a brush in the chocolate and glaze the whole cake. Powder with cocoa. Leave at room temperature for 60 minutes before cutting thin slices with a sharp knife. The cake will be easier to cut if you first dip the knife in hot water.

A section of truffle cake.

Fill the hole with ganache.

Powder with cocoa, using a tea strainer.

Tip

Serve this truffle cake as a dessert, with white chocolate ice cream. The powerful chocolate cake and the mild ice cream make a pleasant combination. See ice cream recipe, Grand Couva p. 168—reduce the sugar by 1.8 oz (50 g) and stir in 6.1 oz (175 g) white chocolate (instead of bittersweet) until it melts.

Chocolate Pain de Gênes   about 10 portions

●

This cake originates from France and could be found in most cake stores until the mid-1960s. It is quick to bake and will keep for at least a week.

A round baking pan, about 9" diameter and 4" high

0.9 oz (25 g) unsalted butter for greasing the pan

1.1 oz (30 g) blanched almond slivers
5.3 oz (150 g) almonds
5.3 oz (150 g) sugar
7 oz (200 g) egg (about 4 eggs)
0.7 oz (20 g) egg yolk (about 1 yolk)
3.2 oz (90 g) unsalted butter
0.5 oz (15 g) all-purpose flour
0.9 oz (25 g) potato flour
2 tsp (10 g) dark rum
0.5 oz (15 g) cocoa powder, preferably Valrhona

1. Grease the pan carefully, using the brush. Throw in the almond slivers. Preheat oven to 350°F.
2. Blanch the whole almonds. Run them in a blender or food processor for about 2 minutes, with the sugar, to make a paste.
3. Scrape the paste into a 2-quart metal bowl and add the egg. Whisk the almond paste, egg yolk and egg to a firm froth, about ten minutes.
4. Melt the butter; it should be about 95°F when added to the mixture.
5. Sieve together the flour and cocoa powder.
6. Fold the flour and rum into the egg mixture. Taking a spoonful, mix it carefully with the melted butter and pour back into the mixture. Blend well until porous.
7. Pour the batter into the baking pan, making sure it comes high up the edges. This will make the resulting cake more even.
8. Bake for 45–50 minutes. The cake should be dry in the middle; use a cake tester to check. Leave in the pan for 5 minutes before turning out onto a rack to cool.

Chocolate Pain de Gênes.

Rehrücken   about 10 portions

● ●

This cake has been one of my favorites for more than
30 years. The name means saddle of venison, reflecting
the shape and pattern of the cake. But you can also bake
it in an ordinary loaf pan.

This is the way we used to make it at the Coba School
in Basel. The cream inside should have a strong flavor of
Kirschwasser.

An oblong pan about 10" long and 2" high, see photo.

Filling
3.5 oz (100 g) almonds
3.5 oz (100 g) sugar
1 lemon
0.9 oz (25 g) cornstarch
3.5 oz (100 g) egg (about 2 eggs), room temperature
3.5 (100 g) butter

Chocolate meringue
butter for greasing the pan
1.1 oz (30 g) almond slivers

3.5 oz (100 g) nuts
0.7 oz (20 g) cornstarch
0.4 oz (10 g) cocoa powder, preferably Valrhona
3.2 oz (90 g) egg white (about 3 whites)
2.1 oz (60 g) sugar
1 tsp freshly squeezed lemon juice
2.1 oz (60 g) sugar

Kirsch cream
1.4 oz (40 g) egg yolk (about 2 yolks)
2.6 oz (75 g) confectioners' flour
1 tbs water
1 vanilla pod
5.3 oz (150 g) unsalted butter, room temperature
1.8 oz (50 g) Kirschwasser or rum (1/4 cup)

DAY 1
Filling
1. Blanch the almonds. Run them in a blender or food processor
   for about 2 minutes with the sugar to make a paste.
2. Mix the almond paste, butter, cornstarch and the peel of half
   a lemon into a creamy paste. Add the eggs, one at a time,
   stirring carefully.

Important!
*The egg must be at room temperature or the paste will
curdle.*

Chocolate meringue
3. Brush the baking pan with soft butter and sprinkle with
   almond slivers. Preheat oven to 400°F. Spread the nuts over
   a baking sheet and roast for about 10 minutes until golden
   brown. Using a tea towel, rub off the skins and remove.
   Grind the nuts as soon as they have cooled.
4. Lower the oven to 350°F. Sift together the cornstarch and
   cocoa powder.
5. Pour egg white, 2.1 oz (60 g) sugar and the lemon juice into
   a metal bowl. Whisk until thoroughly blended.
6. Place the bowl over a saucepan of boiling water. Stir continuously until the mixture reaches 122–140°F.
7. Whisk the meringue until cool, using an electric mixer at low
   speed, or slowly by hand.
8. Carefully fold in the powdered nuts, 2.1 oz (60 g) sugar, flour
   and cocoa using a baking spatula.
9. Spread the meringue around the inside of the pan to make a
   lining.
10. Pour the filling into the lining. Bake for 45–55 minutes. Use a
    needle or wooden pick to check that the inside of the cake is
    dry. Remove from the oven and leave in the baking pan for
    5 minutes before un-panning and placing on a rack. Leave
    overnight or cool in a refrigerator before continuing.

DAY 2 OR LATER THE SAME DAY
Make the Kirsch cream
11. Pour egg yolk, confectioners' sugar and water into a metal
    bowl. Divide the vanilla pod lengthwise and scrape the seeds
    from one half into the bowl.
12. Whisk gently until thoroughly mixed. Place the bowl over a
    saucepan of boiling water. Stir continuously, until 122–140°F.
13. Whisk the egg mixture with an electric mixer until cool.
14. Add the unsalted butter and Kirschwasser. On very low speed,
    whisk for about 10 minutes into a fluffy cream. (This cream is
    often colored pink in Switzerland, which I think is a shame.)
15. Remove the cake from the refrigerator, turn it upside down
    and cut out the wedge from the middle using a sharp knife.
    Lift out the wedge and 3/4 fill the hole with cream. Press the
    wedge back in and leave to stiffen in the refrigerator.
16. Powder with confectioners' sugar. If it's Christmas, you can
    decorate with some chocolate trees; see p. 34.

Rehrücken and Pine Cone.

Pine Cone   12–15 portions

• • •

This scrumptious Christmas cake is a bit tricky to make but is worth the effort, because the cake will keep for the whole holiday.

Meringue mushrooms

2.1 oz (60 g) egg white (about 2 whites)
4.2 oz (120 g) confectioners' sugar
1 tsp freshly squeezed lemon juice
0.4 oz (10 g) cocoa powder, preferably Valrhona

Hazelnut cake base

3.7 oz (105 g) hazelnuts
3.7 oz (105 g) sugar
3.5 oz (100 g) egg (about 2 eggs)
2.1 oz (60 g) egg yolk (about 3 yolks)
1.1 oz (30 g) cornstarch
1.2 oz (35 g) butter
6.3 oz (180 g) egg white (about 6 whites)
1 tsp freshly squeezed lemon juice
1.8 oz (50 g) sugar

Praline cream

7 oz (200 g) almonds
5.6 oz (160 g) sugar
3.5 oz (100 g) water (1/2 cup)

Egg cream

vanilla pod
1 1/2 cups milk
2.1 oz (60 g) egg yolk (about 3 yolks)
2.8 oz (80 g) sugar
17.5 oz (500 g) unsalted butter, room temperature

1 batch hazelnut gianduia, see Chestnuts, p. 73
2.8 oz (80 g) glucose

Meringue mushrooms

1. Preheat oven to 275°F. Pour egg white, confectioners' sugar and lemon juice into a metal bowl. Whisk gently until thoroughly mixed.
2. Place the bowl over a saucepan of boiling water. Stir continuously and bring the mixture to 122–140°F.
3. Using the lowest speed on an electric mixer, or slowly by hand, stir the meringue mixture until cool.
4. Pipe out mushroom hats and mushroom stalks as shown in the photo. Powder with cocoa.
5. Bake for about 60 minutes, turning off the oven after 30 minutes.
6. Before they have stiffened completely, place the hat on the stalks and press gently together. This is a simple and jolly decoration.

Hazelnut cake base

7. Preheat oven to 400°F. Spread the hazelnuts on a baking sheet and roast for about 10 minutes until golden brown. Use a tea towel to rub off the skins and remove. Pulverize the nuts and mix with sugar in a blender or food processor.
8. Raise the oven to 425°F.
9. Whisk the egg, egg yolk and nut sugar (so-called TPT) for about 10 minutes.
10. Sift the cornstarch. Melt the butter.
11. Whisk the egg white, lemon juice and sugar until stiff.
12. Fold the egg-nut mixture and the sifted flour into the egg white.
13. Take a spoonful of the batter and mix it with the melted butter. Pour back into the batter and mix until porous.
14. Using a spatula, spread out the batter completely smoothly, on a baking cloth or parchment paper.
15. Bake for 7–8 minutes.
16. Remove from the oven and immediately lift the cake base from the baking sheet.

Praline cream

17. Preheat oven to 400°F. Roast the un-blanched almonds until golden brown, stirring occasionally.
18. Pour the water into a saucepan, add the sugar and bring to a boil.
19. Remove from the heat when the sugar syrup has reached 230°F. Use a thermometer or do a finger test; see p. 44.
20. Add the almonds and boil until they begin to sputter and pop. Stir occasionally.
21. Stir more vigorously when the sugar begins to whiten and crystallize.
22. Continue stirring until the sugar has melted to golden caramel.
23. Pour out and leave to cool on a baking cloth or parchment paper.
24. Run in a blender or food processor until the paste becomes oily and creamy. Check with a thermometer; it should be about 158°F. Leave to cool.

Egg-cream

25. Divide the vanilla pod lengthwise. Scrape the seeds into a saucepan, add milk and the empty pod.
26. Cream together the egg yolk and sugar. Boil the vanilla milk, remove the pod and add the egg and sugar. Mix thoroughly, before returning to the saucepan.
27. Stirring continuously, heat until the sauce is 185°F. Do a rose or spoon test if you do not have a thermometer; see p. 45. Sieve the sauce into a bowl and cool quickly in a saucepan of cold water.
28. Cream the butter, using an electric mixer at medium speed. Add the cooled egg cream and praline cream. Mix together until light and fluffy.
29. Make a batch of hazelnut gianduia, see Chestnuts p. 73. Add 2.8 oz (80 g) glucose.

Assembling the cake

30. Divide the cake base into three lengths of equal width.
31. Place one length on a baking sheet covered with parchment paper. Spread it with 1/3 of the egg-cream. Place another layer on top and repeat.
32. Put the top layer in place and press together gently. Leave to stiffen in the refrigerator for 60 minutes.
33. Point the cake at both ends using a knife. Round off the corners to give a cone shape. Place the cut off pieces on top and spread over the remaining cream. Leave to stiffen in a refrigerator.

34. Add the glucose and work the gianduia into a pliable paste. Flour a rolling pin with confectioners' sugar and roll out the paste into a sheet, somewhat longer and wider than the cone. Lay the sheet of gianduia over the rolling pin and cover the cone. Press the edges together with your fingers and trim away any excess gianduia.
35. Make gashes with the scissors, from the inside outwards. Powder with confectioners' sugar and decorate with the mushrooms.

The top is cut with scissors.

CHAPTER 8

exotic tartes and cakes

Left: Apricot Tart with Chocolate Chibouste, p. 126.

Chocolate Fondant Cake   8 portions

• •

I have chosen Valrhona Grand Cru Pur Caraïbe 66.5% for this cake. It has a well-rounded, but not too dominant, chocolate flavor. This cake should be somewhat soggy in the middle. See cover photo.

1 baking pan, 9 inch diameter and 1 inch high

0.4 oz (10 g) butter for greasing the pan

Chocolate sablé dough
7.9 oz (225 g) all-purpose flour
0.9 oz (25 g) cocoa powder
5.3 oz (150 g) unsalted butter, room temperature
1 pinch salt
1 tsp (5 g) vanilla sugar
3.5 oz (100 g) confectioners' sugar
0.9 oz (25 g) almond flour, see p. 86
1.8 oz (50 g) egg (1 egg)
0.7 oz (20 g) egg yolk (1 yolk)

Chocolate ganache for filling
8.8 oz (250 g) bittersweet chocolate (Valrhona Grand Cru
    Pur Caraïbe 66.5% or Marabou dark)
8.8 oz (250 g) heavy cream (1 1/8 cup)
3.5 oz (100 g) milk (1/2 cup)
1.8 oz (50 g) egg (1 egg)
0.7 oz (20 g) egg yolk (1 yolk)

1 batch chocolate icing, see chestnut mousse cake, p. 144

Chocolate spiral
3.5 oz (100 g) semisweet chocolate (Valrhona Caraque
    56% or Marabou dark)

Chocolate sablé dough
1. Sift the flour and cocoa in a circle on the work surface. Place the butter, salt, vanilla sugar, confectioners' sugar and almond flour in the middle of the circle.
2. Using your fingertips (or transfer to a blender), work until the mixture resembles breadcrumbs.
3. Add the egg and egg yolk. Work into dough as quickly as possible, by hand or using the blender. Cover with plastic wrap and refrigerate for at least 1 hour.

Lining the baking pan
4. Using your hands, work the chilled dough until it is pliable.
5. Grease the baking pan.
6. Roll out the dough, about 1/4 inch thick, large enough to cover the whole baking pan. Line the pan, and prick the

bottom with a fork. (Any leftover dough can be frozen for another occasion.)
7. Place the baking pan in the freezer for at least 30 minutes.
8. Preheat oven to 350°F.
9. Blind bake the lining for 12 minutes until light brown. Remove from the oven.

Lower oven heat to 300°F.

Ganache filling
10. Finely chop the chocolate.
11. Boil together the milk and cream. Pour over the chopped chocolate and whisk to a smooth and shiny mixture.
12. Whisk the egg and egg yolk into the ganache and pour the ganache into the blind-baked cake lining.
13. Bake in the oven at 300°F for 8–10 minutes.
14. Take out and cool to room temperature.
15. Pour the chocolate icing over the cake and spread out evenly with a spatula.
16. Decorate with a chocolate spiral as in the photo opposite.

Chocolate spiral
Temper the semisweet chocolate and spread, 1/4 inch thick and 1 1/2 inch wide, onto acetate film. Pull a glue scraper towards you to make strips of chocolate, leaving a rim at the top. When the chocolate begins to harden, roll up the film and place it in a tumbler. Leave to harden in a refrigerator. Carefully remove the chocolate from the film.

Tip

Serve this cake at room temperature, never cold, with vanilla ice cream or whipped cream.

Use an ordinary glue scraper to make parallel strips of chocolate, which will then be formed into a spiral by rolling up the film underneath.

Apricot Tarte with Chocolate Chibouste
6–8 portions

• •

This recipe is a version of the classic French clafouti, made with cherries or black morellos in the summer or pears in the autumn. See p. 122.

1 baking pan, about 9 inch diameter, or square as in the photo opposite

0.4 oz (10 g) butter for greasing the pan
1 baking pan, 7 inch diameter, for the chocolate chibouste

Chocolate pastry
8.2 oz (235 g) all-purpose flour
0.5 oz (15 g) cocoa powder, preferably Valrhona
6.7 oz (190 g) unsalted butter
1 tsp (5 g) sugar
1 tsp (5 g) salt
0.7 oz (20 g) egg yolk (1 yolk)
1.8 oz (50 g) milk (1/4 cup)
0.9 oz (25 g) finely chopped, un-blanched almonds

Clafouti filling
2.6 oz (75 g) milk (1/3 cup)
0.5 oz (15 g) heavy cream (1 tbs)
1.6 oz (45 g) raw sugar
1.8 oz (50 g) egg (1 egg)
0.7 oz (20 g) egg yolk (1 yolk)
1 tsp (5 g) cognac
17.5 oz (500 g) apricots

Choclate chibouste
1 gelatin sheet
4.2 oz (120 g) bittersweet chocolate (Valrhona Grand Cru Manjari 64.5% or Marabou dark)
3.2 oz (90 g) egg white (3 whites)
1.8 oz (50 g) sugar
1 tsp freshly squeezed lemon juice
3.5 oz (100 g) milk (1/2 cup)
1.8 oz (50 g) heavy cream (1/4 cup)
about 1 tsp (6 g) cornstarch
2.1 oz (60 g) egg yolk (3 yolks)

confectioners' sugar
cocoa for powdering

Chocolate pastry
This is a stable, delicious pastry, perfectly suited for moist fillings.
1. Sift the flour and cocoa in a circle on the work surface. Place the butter, salt and sugar in the middle of the circle.
2. Using your fingertips or a blender, work until the mixture resembles breadcrumbs.
3. Add the egg, egg yolk and milk. As quickly as possible, work into dough by hand, or using the blender. Cover with plastic wrap and refrigerate for at least 1 hour (or 30 minutes in a freezer).
4. Roll out the dough, about 1/8 inch thick, enough to cover the inside of the baking pan. Line the greased pan with the dough, and prick the bottom with a fork.
5. Place the baking pan in the freezer for 30 minutes to prevent the lining sliding down.
6. Sprinkle lining with the chopped almonds.
7. Slice each apricot into 6 clefts and arrange in the middle of the tart.
8. Preheat oven to 350°F.

Clafouti filling
9. Pour milk, cream, sugar, egg, egg yolk and cognac into a plastic bowl and mix until smooth. Pour the mixture, through a strainer, over the apricots.
10. Bake in the oven for about 40 minutes until golden brown. Take out and leave to cool. The clafouti makes an excellent dessert in itself.

Chocolate chibouste
11. Soak the gelatin sheet in plenty of cold water.
12. Finely chop the chocolate and melt, while stirring, in a microwave oven or double boiler until it has reached 131°F.
13. Put the egg white, sugar and lemon juice in a metal bowl. Whisk lightly until thoroughly mixed.
14. Place the bowl over a saucepan of boiling water and whisk continuously until the mixture has reached 130–140°F.
15. Using an electric mixer at low speed, or slowly by hand, whisk until cool.
16. Pour milk, cream, cornstarch and egg yolks into a small saucepan. Whisk the ingredients together thoroughly.
17. Heat the cream-egg mixture, stirring carefully all the while, until it has boiled.
18. Remove from the heat and add the drained gelatin sheet, stirring until the sheet has melted completely.
19. Add the finely chopped chocolate and stir until completely melted.
20. Pour through a fine strainer.
21. Fold the chocolate cream into the meringue, using a baking spatula. Scrape the mixture into an 7 inch baking ring and smooth the top.
22. Place in the freezer for 30 minutes.
23. Use a knife to remove the chibouste from the baking ring and place it on top of the clafouti tarte. Powder with a little cocoa and confectioners' sugar and leave at room temperature for 30 minutes before serving.

Tips

You can vary the fruit according to season. Cherries, for example, are delicious but don't forget to pit them before use.

Chocolate Tarte   8 portions

• •

I have chosen Valrhona Grand Cru Pur Caraïbe 66.5%, made from trinitario beans, for this tarte. This gives the ganache a mild, well-rounded flavor that is not as dominant as if we had used chocolate with a higher cocoa percentage.

8 tartlet pans, about 4 inch diameter, or 1 large baking pan, 9 inch diameter and 1 inch high.

0.4 oz (10 g) butter for greasing

Almond sablé dough
8.8 oz (250 g) all-purpose flour
5.3 oz (150 g) unsalted butter, room temperature
1/2 tsp (2 g) salt
1 tsp (5 g) vanilla sugar
3.5 oz (100 g) confectioners' sugar
1.2 oz (35 g) almond flour, see p. 86
1.8 oz (50 g) egg (1 egg)
0.7 oz (20 g) egg yolk (1 yolk)

Almond cream with chocolate
0.9 oz (25 g) almonds
0.9 oz (25 g) raw sugar
1 tsp (5 g) cocoa powder
0.9 oz (25 g) unsalted butter
1.4 oz (40 g) egg yolks (2 yolks), room temperature

Ganache
7 oz (200 g) bittersweet chocolate (Valrhona Grand Cru
    Pur Caraïbe 66.5% or Marabou dark)
7 oz (200 g) heavy cream (7/8 cup)
0.9 oz (25 g) honey
1.8 oz (50 g) unsalted butter, room temperature

Decoration, bi-colored fans (see p. 40)
1.8 oz (50 g) white chocolate (Valrhona Ivoire, Lindt,
    Callebaut or Fazer)
1.8 oz (50 g) bittersweet chocolate (Valrhona Grand Cru
    Pur Caraïbe 66.5% or Marabou dark)

cocoa for powdering

Almond sablé dough
1. Sift the flour in a pile on the work surface. Place the butter, salt, vanilla sugar, confectioners' sugar and almond flour in the middle of the pile.

2. Using your fingertips or a blender, work until the mixture resembles breadcrumbs.
3. Add the egg and egg yolk. As quickly as possible, work into dough by hand, or using the blender. Cover with plastic wrap and refrigerate for at least 1 hour.

Lining the tartlet pans (baking pan)
4. Grease the tartlet pans (or 9 inch baking pan).
5. Roll out the dough, about 1/8 inch thick. Press out 4 inch circles of dough, flour the underside and press into the tartlet pans (or 9 inch pan).
6. Prick the tarte linings with a fork. Place in the freezer for at least 30 minutes

Almond cream
8. Pulverize the almonds in a blender or food processor. Mix the almond with the raw sugar and cocoa into a powder, a so-called TPT.
8. Add confectioners' sugar and butter and mix to a creamy paste.
9. Add the egg yolks one at the time, stirring carefully.
10. Preheat oven to 350°F.
11. Fill the tartlet pans (or pan) with the almond cream, using a baking spatula.
12. Bake until golden brown, about 12 minutes for the small tartes and 15 for the large.
13. Remove and leave to cool.

Ganache
14. Finely chop the chocolate and place in a plastic bowl.
15. Boil the cream and honey in a small saucepan and pour it over the chopped chocolate. Stir with a plastic spoon until smooth.
16. Stir in the butter when the mixture has reached 95–105°F. Mix to a creamy ganache using a hand blender.
17. With a spatula, spread the ganache evenly over the tartlets.
18. Leave to stiffen at room temperature, at least 30 minutes.
19. Powder with cocoa and decorate with chocolate fans.
20. Serve with vanilla ice cream and fresh raspberries if you wish.

Tip

These tartes are of course just as tasty without the fans but it's worth taking the trouble to decorate them beautifully. In France they always use a piece of gold leaf!

Chocolate tartelettes   8 portions

● ●

8 tartlet pans, about 4 inch diameter
0.4 oz (10 g) butter for greasing

1 batch almond sablé dough

Almond sablé dough
8.8 oz (250 g) all-purpose flour
5.3 oz (150 g) unsalted butter, room temperature
1/2 tsp (2 g) salt
1 tsp (5 g) vanilla sugar
3.5 oz (100 g) confectioners' sugar
1.2 oz (35 g) almond flour, see p. 86
50 g egg (1 egg)
20 g egg yolk (1 yolk)

1 batch almond cream with chocolate

Almond cream with chocolate
0.9 oz (25 g) almonds
0.9 oz (25 g) raw sugar
1 tsp (5 g) cocoa powder
0.9 oz (25 g) unsalted butter
1.4 oz (40 g) egg yolks (2 yolks), room temperature

Boiled milk chocolate mousse
2.1 oz (60 g) milk chocolate (Valrhona Jivara Lactée 40%
    or Marabou milk chocolate)
7 oz (200 g) heavy cream (7/8 cup)
confectioners' sugar
17.5 oz (500 g) fresh raspberries, strawberries or
    blackberries

Chocolate loops, see p. 39
3.5 oz (100 g) bittersweet chocolate (Valrhona Grand Cru
    Manjari 64.5% or Marabou dark)

1. Prepare the almond sablé dough and line the tartlet pans,
   see Chocolate Tarte, p. 128.
2. Make the almond cream, as for chocolate tarte.

Boiled chocolate mousse
3. Finely chop the chocolate and place in a deep plastic bowl.
4. Boil half the cream and pour over the chopped chocolate.
   Mix until smooth, by hand or using a hand blender.
5. Add the cold cream and mix thoroughly. Leave to chill in the
   refrigerator for at least 3 hours.
6. Make chocolate loops, see p. 39.
7. Bake the tartelettes shortly before eating, see Chocolate Tarte.
8. Whisk the mousse until light and porous, by hand or using an
   electric mixer. Dip a tablespoon in hot water, and scoop out an
   "egg" of mousse. Place a spoonful in each tartelette and
   smooth.
9. Decorate with berries and confectioners' sugar.
10. Carefully loosen the chocolate loops from the plastic film and
    attach one to each mousse.

*When I was a boy at the Savoy Hotel
in Malmö, we used to bake fresh
petits fours for our most discerning
guests. They were placed in baskets
decorated with flowers and rosettes,
all made of caramel. We had a
cupboard with drawers of quicklime,
which we used to draw out the
moisture from the baskets. It was
a tough, hot job weaving all
the baskets for a large order.*

Othello   makes about 12

● ●

This delicious creation has many names. The Germans call it Mohrenkopf and the Austrians Indianerkrapfen. The French and the Swedes know it as Othello meringues, after the famous opera by Giuseppe Verdi.

Othello base

- 2.3 oz (65 g) all-purpose flour
- 1.8 oz (50 g) potato flour
- 5.3 oz (150 g) egg white (about 5 whites)
- 1 tsp freshly squeezed lemon juice
- 1.8 oz (50 g) sugar
- 3.5 oz (100 g) egg yolk (about 5 yolks)

Vanilla cream, crème pâtissière

- 2 cups milk
- 1 vanilla pod
- 4.2 oz (120 g) egg yolk (about 6 yolks)
- 4.4 oz (125 g) sugar
- 1.4 oz (40 g) cornstarch
- 0.7 oz (20 g) unsalted butter

Chocolate glaze

- 4 sheets (8 g) gelatin
- 7.9 oz (225 g) water (1 cup)
- 6.5 oz (185 g) sugar
- 1.4 oz (40 g) glucose
- 2.6 oz (75 g) cocoa powder, preferably Valrhona
- 0.7 oz (20 g) bittersweet chocolate (Valrhona Grand Cru Guanaja 70.5% or Marabou dark)
- 5.3 oz (150 g) heavy cream (3/4 cup)

Glazing is done on a rack.

Apricot gel

7 oz (200 g) apricot jam
2 tbs freshly squeezed lemon juice
1.8 oz (50 g) sugar
1/4 cup water

Othello base

1. Preheat oven to 425°F.
2. Sieve the flour and potato flour on a paper.
3. Whisk the egg white, lemon juice and sugar until stiff.
4. Fold in the egg yolks and flour, using a baking spatula.
5. Using a disposable pastry bag with a smooth no. 12 tip, or cut a largish hole with scissors, pipe out quite large mounds of batter onto parchment paper.
6. Bake for 12 minutes until golden brown and leave to cool somewhat.
7. Turn over the base and hollow out with teaspoon, see photo below.

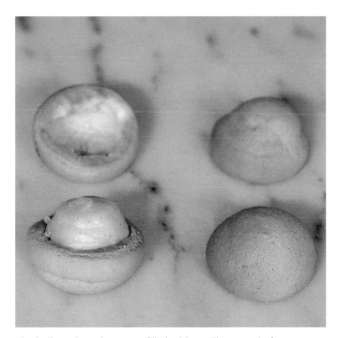

The hollowed-out bases are filled with vanilla cream before sandwiching together.

Vanilla cream

8. Pour the milk into a small, thick-bottomed saucepan.
9. Slice the vanilla pod lengthwise and scrape the seeds into the milk together with the empty pod.
10. Boil the milk. Remove from the heat and leave to draw for 10–15 minutes. Remove the vanilla pod.

11. In a bowl, whisk the egg yolk, sugar and cornstarch until light and frothy.
12. Pour the milk into the egg froth, stirring continuously until completely smooth.
13. Pour the mixture back into the saucepan. Bring back to the boil whisking carefully.
14. Add the butter. Remove from the heat and whisk into a smooth cream.
15. Strain the vanilla cream into a flat container.
16. Chill as quickly as possible in ice cold water. This will ensure the cream keeps better.
17. Wrap in plastic and store in a refrigerator.

Chocolate glaze

18. Soak the gelatin sheets in plenty of cold water.
19. Boil together the water, sugar and glucose. Sift the cocoa and chop the chocolate. Add these to the sugar syrup together with the cream.
20. Bring back to the boil. Lower the heat so that the mixture is simmering, whisk or stir occasionally so that it does not burn. Simmer gently for 1 hour.

    Test, by lifting out the whisk and seeing if drops form on it.

21. Remove and drain the gelatin sheets in a colander. Add the sheets to the chocolate sauce and stir until completely melted.
22. Pour the sauce through a sieve. Cover with plastic wrap to prevent a skin forming. Leave to cool until 95°F, when the glaze will have the right temperature for use.

Apricot gel

23. Boil together all the ingredients for the apricot gel. Simmer on a low heat until the mixture has thickened. Test by dropping a teaspoonful on a plate. After 1 minute, it should be firm and not sticky.

Assembly

24. Stir the vanilla cream until pliable. Fill a pastry bag and pipe a generous amount of cream in the bases.
25. Sandwich in twos and place on a rack.
26. Brush the whole "sandwich" with the warm apricot gel.
27. Heat the chocolate glaze to 95°F, and pour over the "sandwiches."
28. Leave to harden in a refrigerator.
29. Arrange on plates and serve with coffee.

Chocolate Napoleons   10 portions

● ●

These delicious miracles are made of crispy chocolate puff pastry layered with vanilla cream. The perfect dessert to round off a light dinner.

1 batch vanilla cream, see Othello, p. 132

Ganache
2.8 oz (80 g) bittersweet chocolate (Valrhona Grand Cru
   Manjari 64.5% or Marabou dark)
2.8 oz (80 g) heavy cream
0.9 oz (25 g) honey
0.9 oz (25 g) sugar

Quick chocolate puff pastry
4.4 oz (125 g) all-purpose flour
1 tbs (8 g) cocoa powder
4.4 oz (125 g) unsalted butter
1/2 tsp (2 g) salt
0.7 oz (20 g) egg yolk (about 1 yolk)
1/4 cup cold water
1 tsp freshly squeezed lemon juice

1. Make the vanilla cream, see Othello meringues p. 132.

Ganache
2. Finely chop the chocolate and put in a microwave bowl.
3. Pour cream, honey and sugar in a small saucepan. Bring to a boil and pour over the chocolate.
4. Stir with a plastic spoon, or hand blender, until the ganache is smooth and pliable.

Chocolate puff pastry
5. Sieve together the flour and cocoa powder onto the work surface. Add a pinch of salt.
6. Cut the cold butter into small cubes. Work the butter into the cocoa flour until it resembles breadcrumbs.
7. Add egg yolk, water and lemon juice. Work into dough, but with some lumps of butter remaining.
8. Wrap in plastic and leave for 30 minutes in a refrigerator.
9. Roll out 2 "turns," as for ordinary puff pastry. That is, first folding the dough in thirds before rolling out. Return to refrigerator for 30 minutes.
10. Repeat step 9.
11. Roll out the dough to the same size as the baking sheet. Prick densely with a fork and leave the dough for 30 minutes at room temperature.
12. Preheat oven to 350°F. Bake for 30 minutes until the pastry appears well done.
13. Leave to cool on a rack for 10 minutes.
14. Using a ruler and knife, cut the pastry into 3 lengths of equal width. Trim the edges.
15. Place one length of pastry on the work surface and spread it with half the vanilla cream.
16. Place the next length of pastry on top and spread with the remaining cream.
17. Glaze the final length of pastry with the ganache, using a spatula. Cut into 10 equal pieces using a sharp knife.
18. Put the glazed pieces of pastry in top of the prepared length and cut out the 10 Napoleons, using a knife dipped in hot water.

*The Napoleon was created
by that great culinary artist,
Marie Antoine Carême,
using classic puff pastry,
vanilla cream and glaze.*

Chocolate Éclair   makes 10

• •

The classic éclair was very popular when I was young. This chocolate variety is even more scrumptious!

1 batch ganache, see chocolate Napoleon, p. 134

Chocolate pâte à choux
4.7 oz (135 g) all-purpose flour
0.4 oz (10 g) cocoa powder
4.4 oz (125 g) water (2/3 cup)
4.4 oz (125 g) milk (2/3 cup)
1 tsp (5 g) salt
1 tsp (5 g) sugar
4.4 oz (125 g) unsalted butter
8.8 oz (250 g) egg (about 5 eggs)

Chocolate vanilla cream
8.8 oz (250 g) milk (1 cup)
2.6 oz (75 g) heavy cream (1/3 cup)
1/2 vanilla pod
2.1 oz (60 g) egg yolk (about 3 yolks)
1.4 oz (40 g) sugar
0.5 oz (15 g) cornstarch
0.5 oz (15 g) all-purpose flour
2.6 oz (75 g) bittersweet chocolate (Valrhona Grand Cru
    Manjari 64.5% or Marabou dark)
0.9 oz (25 g) unsalted butter

1 batch apricot gel, see Othello, p. 132

1.   Make a batch of ganache; see Chocolate Napoleon, p. 134.

Chocolate pâte à choux
2.   Sift together flour and cocoa on a paper.
3.   Heat up water, milk, salt, sugar and butter in a large saucepan. Bring to a boil, while stirring. Then remove from the heat.
4.   Add all the flour and cocoa in one go. Stir vigorously with a wooden spoon.
5.   Return to the heat. Roast the paste, stirring continuously, until it leaves the edges and forms into a ball.
6.   Leave to cool for 5 minutes.
7.   Preheat oven to 425°F.
8.   Add the eggs one at a time, stirring vigorously between each egg, until the mixture is shiny and creamy.

9.   Using a disposable pastry bag with smooth no. 12 tip (or cut a hole), pipe out narrow, 6 inch lengths on parchment paper.
10. Heat the baking sheet for 5 minutes. The heat will cause the bottom of the éclairs to spread out somewhat, making them more stable.
11. Bake with the oven door closed until the éclairs are light golden, have risen somewhat and stabilized.
12. Open the oven door and bake for a further 20–25 minutes. If you remove them too early they will deflate.
13. Tap the éclairs. If they sound hollow, they are ready. Leave to cool on racks.

Chocolate vanilla cream
14. Pour the milk into a thick-bottomed saucepan.
15. Slice the vanilla pod lengthwise and scrape the seeds into the milk, together with the empty pod.
16. Boil the milk. Remove from the heat and leave to draw for 10–15 minutes. Take out the vanilla pod.
17. In a bowl, whisk the egg yolk, sugar and cornstarch until light.
18. Pour the milk into the egg mixture, stirring continuously until completely smooth.
19. Pour the milk-egg mixture back into the saucepan. Bring back to a vigorous boil, whisking carefully.
20. Chop the chocolate and whisk it into the mixture together with the butter. Whisk to a smooth cream.
21. Strain the cream into a flat container.
22. Chill as quickly as possible, in ice cold water.
23. Pierce a small hole in one end of the éclair. Using a pastry bag with smooth tulle no. 8, insert the pipe in the hole and fill with vanilla cream until the éclair feels full.

Apricot gel
24. Boil the apricot gel; see Othello, p. 132. Brush the top side of the éclairs with gel.
25. Dip the top in the ganache, removing any excess glaze from the edges.
26. Leave to harden in a refrigerator. Serve with coffee, or as a dessert with fruit and white chocolate sorbet.

Left: piped éclair batter and right: ready for eating!

Opéra Cake   about 12–14 portions

● ● ●

This cake was created by a pastry chef in Paris, to celebrate the opening of the old Opera House. It has a wonderful mixture of chocolate, almond and coffee flavors. It can be cut into smaller pieces or petits fours.

Refrigerate the cake for one day, to make it moist, before glazing.

Bisquit Joconde

2 baking sheets, covered with baking cloth or
    parchment paper

8.8 oz (250 g) egg (about 5 eggs)
12.3 oz (350 g) TPT, see p. 86
1.8 oz (50 g) all-purpose flour
1.4 oz (40 g) unsalted butter
11.4 oz (325 g) egg white (about 10 whites)
2 tsp freshly squeezed lemon juice
2.8 oz (80 g) sugar
confectioners' sugar

Coffee butter cream (so-called French butter cream)

13.1 oz (375 g) unsalted butter
1/2 vanilla pod, preferably from Tahiti
2.8 oz (80 g) water (1/3 cup)
6.7 oz (190 g) sugar
0.7 oz (20 g) Nescafé, dark roasted
3.5 oz (100 g) egg yolk (about 5 yolks)

Coffee sugar syrup

7 oz (200 g) water (7/8 cup)
5.3 oz (150 g) sugar
0.7 oz (20 g) Nescafé, dark roasted
1.8 oz (50 g) cognac (1/4 cup)

Opéra glaze

7 oz (200 g) bittersweet chocolate (Valrhona Grand Cru
    Guanaja 70.5% or Marabou dark)
2.6 (75 g) milk (1/3 cup)
1.2 oz (35 g) heavy cream (1/8 cup)
0.9 oz (25 g) honey
0.9 oz (25 g) sugar
0.9 oz (25 g) unsalted butter, room temperature

For brushing the bottom layer

1.8 oz (50 g) bittersweet chocolate (Valrhona Grand Cru
    Guanaja 70.5% or Marabou dark)

DAY 1

Bisquit Joconde

1. Preheat oven to 425°F.
2. Whisk egg and TPT for 10 minutes with an electric mixer.
3. Sieve the flour onto a plate. Melt the butter.
4. Whisk the egg white, lemon juice and sugar until stiff.
5. Using a baking spatula, fold the egg and TPT mixture into the egg white. Fold in the sieved flour.
6. Take a spoonful of the mixture and blend it carefully with the melted butter. Pour back, and mix to a porous batter.
7. Spread the batter in an even layer on a baking cloth, using a spatula.
8. Bake for 7–8 minutes until golden brown.
9. Take out from the oven and immediately remove the bisquit layer from the baking sheet.
10. Powder generously with confectioners' sugar and place on parchment paper.

Preferably bake the bisquit layers the day before you assemble the cake. They will be more stable and easy to work with. Bisquit layers can be frozen if you wish.

Coffee butter cream

11. Cream the butter until light and fluffy, almost like whipped cream.
12. Slice the half vanilla pod and scrape the seeds into a saucepan.
13. Add water, sugar and Nescafé and stir until dissolved.
14. Bring to a boil. Dip a brush in cold water and brush down any crystals formed on the sides of the saucepan.
15. Whisk the egg yolks until frothy, using an electric mixer, while the syrup is boiling.
16. When the sugar syrup has reached 243°F, pour it into the egg yolk mixture, stirring continuously. If you do not have a thermometer for the sugar syrup, do a finger test; see p. 44.
17. Whisk at a low speed until the egg mixture has cooled. You can speed this process by placing the saucepan in a bowl of cold water while you whisk.
18. Add the fluffed butter to the egg mixture and blend to a porous butter cream.

Coffee sugar syrup

19. Mix the water, sugar and Nescafé in a saucepan and bring to a boil. Leave to cool.
20. Add cognac and mix.

Recipe continues on next page.

Opéra glaze

21. Finely chop the 7 oz (200 g) chocolate and put in a plastic bowl.
22. Pour milk, cream, honey and sugar into a small saucepan. Bring to a boil while stirring. Pour over the chocolate and mix with a plastic spoon, or hand blender, into a smooth and pliable ganache. Stir in the butter.
23. Cover the bowl with plastic wrap. Leave overnight at room temperature.
24. Finely chop the 1.8 oz (50 g) chocolate (to be used for brushing the bottom layer) into a plastic bowl. Melt in a microwave oven, stirring occasionally, to 130°F.

DAY 1

Assembling the cake

25. Trim the bisquit layers with a knife. Place them on top of each other and cut them lengthwise into 4 equal pieces.
26. Turn the first piece onto parchment paper. Brush with the melted chocolate, right out to the edges.
27. Place a parchment paper on top, and turn over onto a baking sheet.
28. Spread 1/3 of the coffee butter cream on the first layer and place the next layer on top.

29. Dip a brush in the coffee sugar syrup and drench the layer with half the syrup.
30. Repeat steps 28 and 29 with the next layer.
31. Repeat the procedure a final time. Place a sheet of parchment paper on top and press with a baking sheet to make the cake completely flat.
32. Brush with the remaining coffee syrup and cover the cake with plastic wrap. Leave to draw overnight. The cake can be frozen at this stage if you wish.

DAY 2 (WHEN SERVING)

33. Heat the Opéra glaze to 95°F, using a microwave oven or double boiler. Do not stir after the glaze is hot or it will lose its shine.
34. Remove the plastic wrap from the cake and pour glaze out over the middle. Spread with a spatula.
35. If you are feeling artistic, you can pipe the word "opéra" on top.
36. Fill a measuring jug with hot water, and dip the knife in it before trimming the edges of the cake, to reveal the layers.

Tip

Serve chilled from the refrigerator. It will soon be a firm favorite! Particularly suitable for long weekends or holidays, since it keeps for several days.

Tarragon Cake with fresh fruit

about 12–14 portions

• • •

**A journey through Italy gave me the inspiration for this
fantastic cake.**

**Creamy hazelnut brûlée, tangy chocolate base,
smooth lemon-flavored mousse encased with white
chocolate and filled with lots of fresh fruit—mmmm!
This cake is really worth the effort.**

Ring of acetate film, 9 1/2 inch diameter

Aluminum foil container, 8 inch diameter, about 1/2-quart

Hazelnut brûlée

2.8 oz (80 g) hazelnuts
7 oz (200 g) heavy cream (7/8 cup)
5.3 oz (150 g) milk (3/4 cup)
1 vanilla pod
2.5 oz (70 g) sugar
4.2 oz (120 g) egg yolk (about 6 yolks)

Chocolate base (without flour)

grated peel of 1/2 lemon
1.4 oz (40 g) egg yolk (about 2 yolks)
0.9 oz (25 g) sugar
0.6 oz (18 g) cocoa powder, preferably Valrhona
2.1 oz (60 g) egg white
1.2 oz (35 g) sugar
1 tsp lemon juice

Milk chocolate mousse

1 sheet gelatin
7 oz (200 g) milk chocolate (Valrhona Jivara Lactée 40% or
    Marabou milk chocolate)
7 oz (200 g) heavy cream (7/8 cup)
2.8 oz (80 g) egg yolk (about 4 yolks)
1.8 oz (50 g) confectioners' sugar
1 tbs Cointreau

For wrapping the cake

1.8 oz (50 g) bittersweet chocolate (Valrhona Grand Cru
    Manjari 64.5% or Marabou dark)
5.3 oz (150 g) white chocolate (Valrhona Ivoire, Callebaut,
    Lindt or Fazer)

For decoration

17.5 oz (500 g) mixed fruit and berries, such as
    raspberries, strawberries, cherries and red currants

DAY 1

Hazelnut brûlée

1. Preheat oven to 400°F.
2. Spread the hazelnuts over a baking sheet and roast for about
   10 minutes until golden brown, stirring occasionally. Rub off
   the skins with a tea towel and put the nuts aside.
3. Lower heat to 205°F.
4. Boil together the cream, milk, vanilla seeds and half the sugar,
   stirring continuously.
5. Whisk the egg yolk and remaining sugar until the mixtures
   lightens and becomes frothy.
6. Strain the boiled cream mixture into the egg froth.
7. Pour 1/4 of the resulting mixture into a blender with the roasted
   hazelnuts and blend until smooth.
8. Pour into an aluminum foil container (about 8 inch diameter
   and 1/2-quart capacity).
9. Place the container in a bowl of cold water and place in the
   oven for 45–60 minutes. Use a cake tester to check that the
   brûlée has the desired firm consistency. Leave to cool.
10. Put the brûlée in a plastic bag and freeze for 24 hours.

Recipe continues on next page.

DAY 2

Chocolate base

11. Preheat oven to 425°F.
12. Make a chocolate base with lemon but no flour.
13. Rinse the lemon thoroughly and grate 1/2 the peel.
14. With a pencil, draw a 8 inch diameter circle on parchment paper.
15. Whisk the egg yolk, 0.9 oz (25 g) sugar and grated lemon peel until frothy.
16. Sift the cocoa onto parchment paper.
17. Whisk the egg white, 1.2 oz (35 g) sugar and lemon juice until stiff.
18. Using a baking spatula, fold the egg yolk mixture and cocoa into the egg white.
19. Spread the batter into the parchment paper circle.
20. Bake the base for 10–12 minutes. Leave to cool on a rack.

Chocolate mousse

21. Soak the gelatin sheet in plenty of cold water for at least 10 minutes.
22. Finely chop the chocolate and melt while stirring, in a microwave oven or double boiler. Heat to 130°F.
23. Lightly whip the cream and refrigerate.
24. Whisk together the egg yolks, confectioners' sugar and Cointreau.
25. Placing the bowl in a saucepan of boiling water, whisk the egg mixture to a creamy paste, about 185°F.
26. Remove from the heat and continue whisking until cool.
27. Mix the chocolate with 1/3 of the lightly whipped cream to a ganache.
28. Drain the gelatin sheet and heat to 105°F, in a microwave oven or over boiling water, until it has melted.
29. Fold the gelatin into the ganache with a baking spatula. Pour in the remaining cream and finally the egg mixture. Blend to a light and porous mousse.
30. Cut out a 2 inch wide strip of acetate film, 30 1/2 inch long. Form into a 9 1/2 inch diameter ring (or use a metal ring).
31. Place the ring on a sheet of acetate film.
32. Pipe out half of the mousse into the ring, using a pastry bag with a no. 10 tip.
33. Take the brûlée out of the freezer and remove from the container. (Push down the brûlée in the middle and it will rise over the edge.)
34. Pipe over with the remaining mousse. Cover with chocolate base. Place the cake in a plastic bag and freeze for at least 2 hours. The cake can be stored up to 2 weeks in the freezer.

LATER DAY 2

35. Take the cake out of the freezer and remove the ring.
36. Cut out a strip of soft plastic film, 2 3/4 inch wide and 31 inch long.
37. Heat both kinds of chocolate to 95°F, using a microwave oven or double boiler.
38. With a spoon, make stripes of dark chocolate on the film. Spread the white chocolate over the film, leaving about 1/2 inch free from chocolate at one end.
39. Immediately place the strip of film around the cake, pressing gently so that stays in place. Chill in the refrigerator for 10 minutes. Remove the plastic film.
40. Fill the hole in the middle with fresh fruit and berries.

Carefully remove the plastic film from the chilled cake.

Cardinal Cakes   makes 10 pieces

• •

This fantastic and easy to make Austrian creation is, unfortunately, not well known in Sweden. I got this recipe from Karl Schumacher, the world-famous head pastry chef at Café Oberlau in Vienna.

Chocolate mousse filling
2.8 oz (80 g) bittersweet chocolate (Valrhona Grand Cru Pur Caraïbe 66.5 % or Marabou dark)
1.4 oz (40 g) egg yolk (about 2 yolks)
10.5 oz (300 g) heavy cream (1 1/4 cups)

Meringue
8.8 oz (250 g) egg white (about 8 whites)
1 tsp freshly squeezed lemon juice
6.3 oz (180 g) sugar

Sponge base
3.5 oz (100 g) egg (about 2 eggs)
2.1 oz (60 g) egg yolk (about 3 yolks)
1.8 oz (50 g) sugar
1 tsp (5 g) real vanilla sugar
1.9 oz (55 g) all-purpose flour

confectioners' sugar

Chocolate mousse filling
1. Finely chop the chocolate and melt in a microwave bowl, or double boiler, until it reaches 130°F (use a thermometer).
2. Stir the egg yolk into the chocolate, using a baking spatula.
3. Whisk the cream until frothy. Fold half the cream into the chocolate, stirring vigorously. Add the remaining cream and mix to a light, porous mousse.

Use a tea strainer when powdering with confectioners' sugar.

Meringue and sponge base
4. Using a pencil, draw two 6 inch wide strips across a piece of parchment paper.
5. Preheat oven to 350°F.
6. Whisk the egg white and lemon juice until the froth begins to lift.
7. Pour in half the sugar and stir with an electric mixer at medium speed, or by hand.
8. Pour in the remaining sugar, stirring continuously. Increase to maximum speed and whisk into a stiff lather.
9. Transfer the meringue batter to a disposable pastry bag, with a large smooth tip (or cut a large hole).
10. Firstly pipe a straight length of meringue in the middle of the strip you have drawn on the parchment paper, and then one length on each edge of the strip. See photo below.

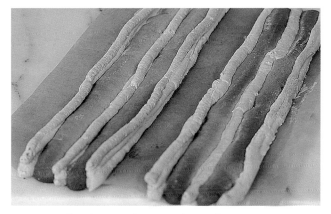

Pipe strips of meringue and sponge alternately.

11. Whisk the egg, sugar, egg yolk and vanilla sugar to a firm froth, using an electric mixer.
12. Sieve the flour and fold it carefully into the egg mixture, using a baking spatula.
13. Using the same pastry bag, pipe the sponge batter between the lines of meringue. Powder lightly with confectioners' sugar.
14. Bake for about 12 minutes until they are light brown. Cool immediately on racks.
15. Divide one of the strips of cake base into 10 equal pieces, 1 1/2 inch wide, using a sharp knife.
16. Place the other strip of cake on the work surface and spread it with chocolate mousse. Smooth with a spatula.
17. Place the 10 cut pieces of cake on top and press down gently. Dipping a sharp knife in hot water, cut through the mousse and cake base. Powder each cake with a little confectioners' sugar.

Tip

These taste at their very best with a mug of hot cocoa after a day's skiing!

Chestnut Cake   14–16 portions

● ● ●

This delicious autumn cake tastes fantastic after a meal of game and robust red wine.

The famous Gerbaud patisserie, from Budapest, made a guest appearance in 2001 at NK in Stockholm. The Hungarian pastry chefs specialized in making chestnut cakes, which sold out very quickly!

The cake can be assembled and stored for several days if carefully wrapped in plastic. Make the marbled chocolate tiles and chestnut petits fours for decoration on the day of serving.

Chocolate base (classic chocolate sponge)
Round pie pan or adjustable ring, 9 1/2 inch diameter

5.3 oz (150 g) egg (about 3 eggs)
2.1 oz (60 g) egg yolk (about 3 yolks)
4 oz (115 g) sugar
1 tsp (5 g) vanilla sugar
1.1 oz (30 g) unsalted butter
3.5 oz (100 g) all-purpose flour
0.9 oz (25 g) cocoa powder, preferably Valrhona

Caramel mousse
2 sheets gelatin (4 g)
1.6 oz (45 g) sugar
0.7 oz (20 g) glucose
0.5 oz (15 g) unsalted butter
1.8 oz (50 g) heavy cream (1/4 cup)
1.4 oz (40 g) egg yolks (about 2 yolks)
4.4 oz (125 g) whipped cream (2/3 cup)

Chestnut mousse
2 sheets gelatin (4 g)
1.8 oz (50 g) egg (about 1 egg)
0.7 oz (20 g) egg yolk (about 1 yolk)
1.8 oz (50 g) confectioners' sugar
8.8 oz (250 g) unsweetened chestnut purée (1 jar)
1 1/2 tbs (25 g) dark rum
8.8 oz (250 g) heavy cream (1 cup)

For assembly: acetate film or a 10 1/2 inch adjustable cake ring.

For decoration and glazing
1.8 oz (50 g) white chocolate (Valrhona Ivoire, Callebaut, Lindt or Fazer)
2.6 oz (75 g) semisweet chocolate (Valrhona Caraque 56% or Marabou dark)
1 batch Opéra glaze; see Opéra cake, p. 137
1 batch Chestnut petits fours; see Petits Fours, p. 92

DAY 1
Make the chocolate sponge
1. Preheat oven to 400°C. Heat water in a large saucepan.
2. Lightly whisk egg, egg yolk, sugar, and vanilla sugar. Place the bowl in the saucepan of boiling water and whisk until the mixture reaches 105°F.
3. Whisk, preferably with an electric mixer, until the batter has cooled. Do not whisk too fast or the batter will loose its volume.
4. Melt the butter in a microwave, or a small saucepan, and put to one side.
5. Sieve flour and cocoa powder onto a sheet of paper.
6. Carefully fold into the batter ensuring that it remains light and porous. Take a spoonful of the batter and mix carefully with the melted butter. Pour back into the batter and blend well, keeping it light.
7. Pour the batter into the baking pan, brushing it up the edges to ensure a more even cake.
8. Bake for 25–30 minutes with the oven ventilator open. Use a cake tester to check that the cake is ready.
9. Sprinkle with sugar, place a sheet of parchment paper on top of the cake. Turn over onto a rack and leave to cool in the baking pan.

Storage
A carefully wrapped sponge can keep for two weeks in the freezer.

Caramel mousse
10. Soak the gelatin in plenty of cold water for 10 minutes.
11. Melt the sugar and glucose in a saucepan, until golden yellow. When a thin "mist" has formed on the surface, quickly add the butter. Remove from the heat and stir.
12. Whisk together the cream and egg yolk in a bowl. Add the caramel and stir thoroughly.
13. Place the bowl in a saucepan of simmering water. Whisk vigorously until the creamy mixture has reached 185°F.
14. Take out the gelatin from the water and stir into the mixture, until completely melted.
15. Press the creamy mixture through a fine sieve into a bowl. Place the bowl a saucepan of cold water and cool to 68°F.
16. Whisk the cream and fold it into the mixture, using a baking spatula.
17. Pour the mousse into a 1/2-quart aluminum container, 8 inch diameter.
18. Freeze for at least 3 hours.

Chestnut mousse

19. Soak the gelatin in plenty of cold water for 10 minutes.
20. Whisk the egg, egg yolk and confectioners' sugar until frothy, using an electric mixer.
21. Add the chestnut purée and rum, mix until smooth.
22. Drain the gelatin sheets and melt them in a microwave oven to 104–122°F. Stir the gelatin into the cream mixture, using a baking spatula.
23. Whisk the cream and fold it into a mixture.

Recipe continues on following page.

DAY 2, OR LATER THE SAME DAY
Assembly
24. Cut out a strip of acetate film, 2 inch wide and 32 inch long. Form into a 10 1/2 inch diameter ring and fasten with staples, or use an adjustable cake ring.
25. Place the ring on a sheet of acetate film. Cut the sponge into 3 equally thick layers and place one layer inside the ring. Pipe in half the chestnut mousse, using a no. 10 smooth tip.
26. Remove the caramel mousse from the aluminum container. Press the caramel mousse into the chestnut mousse so that the chestnut mousse is squeezed up the edges. Pipe out the remaining chestnut mousse and place the second cake layer on top. Freeze the third layer for another occasion.

Decoration and glazing
27. Melt 1.8 oz (50 g) white chocolate. Dip a clean dish brush into the white chocolate, and spread backwards and forwards on a sheet of acetate film until it begins to harden.

28. Temper the semisweet chocolate and spread half over the white chocolate. Spread backwards and forwards with a spatula. Leave in a refrigerator to harden. Spread the remaining semisweet chocolate evenly over a half sheet of acetate film. Using a glue scraper, make chocolate loops; see p. 34. Roll up the acetate film and place in a refrigerator.
29. Heat the Opéra glaze in a microwave oven to 95°F.
30. Loosen the ring of plastic from the frozen cake.
31. Place the cake on an upturned tin in the middle of a sheet of parchment paper. Firstly pour the glaze round the edge of the cake. Then pour the remaining glaze into the middle and spread out over the whole cake with one sweep of a spatula. Allow the glaze to drip for 5 minutes.
32. Transfer the cake to a large plate. Decorate the edges with marbled chocolate tiles that you break off from the acetate film.
33. Decorate the top with glazed chestnut petits fours and some chocolate loops from the other piece of acetate film; see p. 34. Leave to defrost in a refrigerator for about 4 hours before serving.

The chocolate ganache is firstly poured round the edges of the frozen cake, which stands on a metal tin.

Glaze the top with a single sweep of the spatula to make a really smooth surface.

Marbled Chocolate Cake with Apple and Calvados   12–14 portions

• • •

This exquisitely glazed chocolate cake is something really special for an autumn or winter dinner. You can prepare and freeze the cake several weeks before you glaze and decorate it. See photo, p. 150.

1 batch chocolate cake sponge, see Chestnut Cake, p. 144

6 green apples, about 1 lb
0.9 oz (25 g) unsalted butter
2.6 oz (75 g) raw sugar
3 tbs (50 g) Calvados, for flambéing

Sugar syrup with Calvados
3.5 oz (100 g) Calvados (1/2 cup)
2.6 oz (75 g) confectioners' sugar
1 1/2 tbs oz (25 g) water

Milk chocolate mousse with Calvados
2 sheets gelatin (4 g)
14 oz (400 g) milk chocolate (Valrhona Jivara Lactée 40% or Marabou milk chocolate)
14 oz (400 g) heavy cream (1 3/4 cups)
4.2 oz (120 g) egg yolk (about 6 yolks)
3.5 oz (100 g) confectioners' sugar
3 tbs (50 g) Calvados

White chocolate glaze
1 sheet gelatin (2 g)
2.6 oz (75 g) white chocolate (Valrhona Ivoire Callebout, Fazer or Lindt)
3 tbs (50 g) milk
0.9 oz (25 g) glucose
0.4 oz (10 g) unsalted butter

1 batch chocolate glaze, see Othello p. 132

Chocolate tiles
1 sheet acetate film
2.6 oz (75 g) semisweet chocolate (Valrhona Caraque 56% or Marabou dark)

DAY 1
1. Make the chocolate sponge as for Chestnut Cake, p. 144.

Caramelized apples
2. Peel and divide the apples into small segments. Heat the butter and raw sugar in a large frying pan. Stir until the sugar caramelizes. Meanwhile, heat the apple segments in a microwave oven, then add to the frying pan and fry until golden brown. Flambé with Calvados, to flavor the apple. Leave to cool on parchment paper.

Making sugar syrup
3. Using a hand blender, mix the Calvados, confectioners' sugar and water in a glass, until the sugar has dissolved.

Milk chocolate mousse with Calvados
4. Soak the gelatin in cold water for about 10 minutes.
5. Finely chop the chocolate and melt to 122°F, in a microwave oven or a double boiler.
6. Lightly whip the cream and refrigerate.
7. Whisk together the egg yolk and confectioners' sugar in a bowl.
8. Place the bowl in a saucepan of simmering water.
9. Whisk vigorously until a creamy batter is formed. Whisk the batter until cool, using an electric mixer or by hand. Mix 1/3 of the whipped cream with the chocolate to make ganache. Drain the gelatin and melt it in a microwave oven or double boiler to 104–122°F. Add Calvados and mix thoroughly. Fold into the ganache. Add the rest of the cream, and finally the batter and mix to a light, porous mousse.

White chocolate gel
10. Soak the gelatin in cold water for about 10 minutes.
11. Finely chop the chocolate and melt to 122°F, in a microwave oven or double boiler.
12. Boil together milk and glucose and pour over the chocolate. Stir to a stiff ganache, using a spoon or hand blender.
13. Stir in the butter.
14. Drain the gelatin sheets and melt to 104–122°F, in a microwave oven or double boiler. Pour into the ganache and mix thoroughly. Cover with plastic wrap and store in a refrigerator or freezer until needed.
    (If you want the gel to be really white, add 1 tsp (5 g) white artificial coloring—titanium oxide.)

15. Make a batch of chocolate glaze, see Othello p. 132.

Chocolate tiles
16. Melt and temper the chocolate; see p. 35. Spread thinly on a sheet of acetate film and leave to harden in a refrigerator.

Recipe continues on following page.

Assembling the cake

17. Cut a long strip of acetate film, 2 inch wide and 32 inch long. Form into a 10 1/2 inch diameter ring (or you can use a metal cake ring).
18. Divide the sponge into 3 equally thick layers, using a serrated knife.
19. Place the ring of plastic on a sheet of acetate film (or use a metal cake ring). Place a layer of sponge in the ring and brush lightly with sugar syrup. Using a smooth no. 10 tip, pipe out a third of the chocolate mousse and spread evenly over the sponge with a baking spatula.
20. Put the next layer in place and soak thoroughly with sugar syrup, saving 1 tbs for the final layer. Spread the caramelized apple segments over the layer. Pipe out the remaining mousse and smooth with a spatula. Put the final layer in place and press down carefully, using a plate, to make the cake even. Brush with the remaining sugar syrup.
21. Put the cake in a plastic bag and freeze overnight. The cake can keep for two weeks in the freezer.

DAY 2 OR LATER

22. Heat both the glazes in a microwave oven or double boiler, stirring until they reach 95°F.
23. Take the cake out of the freezer and remove the plastic ring (or unpan). Place it on a tin, with parchment paper underneath. Pour the dark glaze around the edge of the cake and the white glaze in the middle. Sweep the glaze backwards and forwards a couple of times to achieve a beautiful marbling effect. Allow the glaze to drip for 5 minutes.
24. Place the cake on a large plate. Decorate the edge with the chocolate tiles from the sheet of acetate film. You can also decorate with a couple of chocolate fans; see p. 40.
25. Let the cake defrost for 4 hours in a refrigerator before serving.

Bishop's Miter—Raspberry and Chocolate Mousse Cake   4 portions

• •

Magnus Johansson, Operakällaren's head pastry chef, and I once used Chuao chocolate (1999 vintage) to make raspberry chocolate mousse when we were on tour with the Dessert Academy in 2001. Our participants waxed lyrical over this combination of raspberry and chocolate. See photo, p. 151.

For the bishop's miter
Cut 4 strips of acetate film, 8 1/2 inch long and 2 3/4 inch wide

Raspberry chocolate mousse
   3 oz (85 g) raspberry purée with 10% sugar (5.3 oz frozen raspberries and about 0.5 oz sugar)
   1/2 sheet gelatin (1 g)
   3.5 oz (100 g) bittersweet chocolate (Valrhona Chuao 65% or Marabou dark)
   3.5 oz (100 g) heavy cream (1/2 cup)
   1.4 oz (40 g) egg yolk (about 2 yolks)
   1.1 oz (30 g) sugar
   0.4 oz (10 g) French raspberry liquor (2 tsp)

Rice Crispies base
   0.7 oz (20 g) almond flakes
   0.5 oz (15 g) confectioners' sugar
   1.8 oz (50 g) milk chocolate (Valrhona Jivara Lactée 40% or Marabou milk)
   0.7 oz (20 g) Rice Crispies (Kellogg's)
   2.6 oz (75 g) bittersweet chocolate (Valrhona Chuao 65% or Marabou dark)
   12 fresh or frozen raspberries
   1 tbs sugar

DAY 1
Raspberry chocolate mousse
1. Mix the raspberries with the sugar, then pass through a sieve.
2. Soak the gelatin in cold water for about 10 minutes.
3. Chop the chocolate and melt to 130°F, in a microwave oven or double boiler.
4. Whip the cream and place in the refrigerator.
5. Whisk together the egg yolk, sugar and raspberry liquor in a bowl. Place the bowl in a saucepan of simmering water. Whisk vigorously until creamy. Remove the bowl and continue whisking until cool, using an electric mixer or by hand.
6. Mix the melted chocolate and raspberry purée. Using a baking spatula, mix to a smooth ganache.
7. Drain the gelatin and melt in a microwave oven, or double boiler. When it has reached 104–122°F, pour the gelatin into the ganache.
8. Fold the ganache, and finally the egg-sugar mixture, into the whipped cream.

Rice Crispies base
9. Preheat oven to 400°F. Spread the almond flakes over a baking sheet and roast for 5 minutes until golden brown, stirring often to avoid burning.
10. Pour the confectioners' sugar and almond flakes into a blender or food processor (or preferably an electric coffee grinder). Mix for 11 minutes to a creamy paste.
11. Add the finely chopped chocolate and mix until it has melted.
12. Pour the mixture over a cold surface and temper (as for chocolate).
13. When it begins to thicken, scrape into a bowl and stir in the Rice Crispies.

14. Cut 4 strips of acetate film, 2 inch wide and 8 1/2 inch long. Staple the strips into 4 rings.
15. Spoon out Rice Crispies base equally in each ring.

Assembling the cakes

16. Place the rings with their Rice Crispies bases on parchment paper. Using a smooth no. 10 tip, pipe out chocolate mousse to half fill the rings. Place 3 raspberries rolled in sugar in each ring and top up with mousse. Refrigerate for at least 3 hours or overnight.

DAY 2 OR LATER THE SAME DAY

17. Chop and melt the chocolate, in a microwave oven or double boiler.

18. Spread a thin layer of chocolate on the strips of acetate film, saving 1 inch at one end.
19. Take the mousse out of the freezer and remove the plastic ring. Encircle the mousse with the strip of chocolate, pressing together in the middle to resemble a bishop's miter; see photo. Place in the freezer for 5 minutes so that the chocolate hardens (crystallizes) and shrinks. Take out from the freezer and carefully remove the plastic film, making sure that the chocolate does not crack. Remove the miters from the freezer one at a time to prevent the film adhering to the chocolate when it warms up.
20. Place in the refrigerator for 2 hours.
21. Serve on a plate.

The plastic is carefully removed from the bishop's miter.

Marbled Chocolate Cake with Apple and Calvados, p. 147.

Bishop's Miter filled with raspberry and chocolate mousse; see p. 148.

Chocolate Mousse cloaked in Gran Couva

4 portions

• • •

This luscious, melting chocolate dessert is a chocophile's dream. Pure chocolate, flavored with chili and tequila. It's enough to transport you to Mexico…

Nils Stormby, chairman of the Swedish Chocolate Academy is particularly enamored with the South American preference for combining chocolate and chili.

Walnut bases

0.9 oz (25 g) almond
0.9 oz (25 g) walnuts
1.8 oz (50 g) sugar
1 tsp (5 g) Nescafé, dark roasted
1.1 oz (30 g) egg white (about 1 white)

2 tbs (25 g) brown Mexican tequila

Gran Couva chocolate mousse

1 tsp roasted chili, seedless jalapeño
5.3 oz (150 g) bittersweet chocolate (Valrhona Gran Couva 68% or Marabou dark)
7 oz (200 g) heavy cream (7/8 cup)
2.8 oz (80 g) egg yolk (about 4 yolks)
1.6 oz (45 g) sugar
1 1/2 tbs (20 g) water

3.5 oz (100 g) bittersweet chocolate (Valrhona Gran Couva 68% or Marabou dark)

Walnut bases

1. Mix to a fine powder the almonds, walnuts, sugar and Nescafé in a food processor. Transfer to a bowl and add the egg white. Stir to a smooth paste, using a baking spatula, and leave to swell for 30 minutes.
2. Preheat oven to 350°F.
3. Pipe 8 bases onto parchment paper.
4. Bake for about 8 minutes until golden brown.
5. Leave to cool on a rack.

Chocolate mousse

6. In a dry frying pan at a low temperature, roast the chili until it is just beginning to melt. Pulverize the chili in a mortar. Chop the chocolate and heat it to 130°F, in a microwave oven or double boiler. Whip the cream until it begins to froth up, then refrigerate.
7. Whisk together the egg yolks, sugar and water in a bowl. Place in a saucepan of simmering water and whisk vigorously to a creamy mixture, 185°F.
8. Pass the mixture through a fine strainer and continue to whisk until cool, using an electric mixer or by hand.
9. Mix to a smooth ganache the chocolate, the chili powder and 1/3 of the whipped cream.
10. Add the remaining cream and egg yolk mixture and blend to a light, porous mousse.
11. Cut 4 strips of acetate film, 2 inch wide and 9 1/2 inch long. Form into 4 rings, stapling the ends together.
12. Place the walnut bases in tequila so that they absorb the liquor. Put a walnut base in each ring and half fill the ring with mousse. Place the other walnut bases on top and fill up the rings with mousse. Freeze for at least 3 hours or overnight.
13. Place a clean baking sheet (or stainless steel tray) in the oven. Set the oven to 104–122°F.
14. Chop the chocolate and heat to 130°F, in a microwave oven or double boiler.
15. Remove the baking sheet from the oven. Spread the melted chocolate thinly end evenly over the whole sheet. Professionals often use a paint roller to get the chocolate really even. Leave the baking sheet in a refrigerator for about 10 minutes.
16. Remove the baking sheet and let the chocolate soften at room temperature.
17. Take out the chocolate mousse, remove the plastic rings and replace in the freezer.
18. Remove one mousse at a time from the freezer. Using a spatula, form a strip of chocolate and encase the mousse with it. Form a circle of chocolate and place on top of the mousse. Move the cake to a plate and encase the other three mousses with chocolate. If the chocolate becomes too soft, refrigerate for a few minutes, then continue working.

Passion Fruit and Chocolate Bavaroise encased with White Chocolate   4 portions

• •

The sharp flavor of Manjari chocolate is well suited to this fruity dessert, with its melting chocolate Bavaroise and beautiful case of ivory chocolate filled with fresh berries. See photo, p. 156.

    4 strips of acetate film, 2 3/4 inch wide and
        8 1/2 inch long

    2.6 oz (75 g) white chocolate (Valrhona Ivoire, Callebaut,
        Lindt or Fazer)
    0.4 oz (10 g) semisweet chocolate
    about 12 passion fruit

Bavaroise
    1.8 oz (50 g) passion fruit purée
    1 sheet gelatin (2 g)
    1.4 oz (40 g) egg yolk (about 2 yolks)
    2.5 oz (70 g) sugar
    2.6 oz (75 g) milk (1/3 cup)
    2.6 oz (75 g) bittersweet chocolate (Valrhona Grand Cru
        Manjari 64.5% or Marabou dark)
    4.4 oz (125 g) heavy cream (2/3 cup)

    7 oz (200 g) mixed soft fruit and berries
    confectioners' sugar

1. Cut out 4 strips of acetate film, 2 3/4 inch wide and 8 1/2 inch long.
2. Melt the white chocolate, in a microwave oven or double boiler. Temper; see p. 35.
3. Melt 0.4 oz (10 g) semisweet chocolate. Dip a teaspoon in the chocolate and draw thin lines of chocolate on the strips of film.
4. Spread a thin layer of white chocolate over the strips of film, leaving 1/2 inch free at one end. Form the strips into rings, placing on a sheet of acetate film. Refrigerate for 30 minutes until hardened.

Bavaroise
5. Divide the passion fruit and pass through a fine strainer. Weigh up 50 g fruit purée.
6. Soak the gelatin sheet, in plenty of cold water, for 10 minutes.
7. Whisk together the passion fruit purée, egg yolk, sugar and milk in a saucepan.
8. Stirring continuously with a wooden spoon, heat carefully until the sauce begins to thicken, about 185°F. Do a rose or spoon test; see p. 45, if you do not have a thermometer.
9. Press through a fine strainer.

10. Drain the sheet of gelatin and add to the hot sauce. Stir until the gelatin has dissolved completely.
11. Finely chop the chocolate, add to the sauce and stir until melted.
12. Cool the sauce to 68°F. Whip the cream. Fold in the chocolate sauce, with a baking spatula. Add half the sauce at a time to prevent the Bavaroise becoming lumpy.
13. Spoon the cream into the chocolate ring and refrigerate for at least 1 hour.
14. Arrange the cakes on plates and remove the plastic film. Fill generously with red soft fruit and berries. Powder with confectioners' sugar.

Autumn Dessert   4 portions

• •

An exquisite dessert with chocolate mousse, black currant mousse and apple sauce. An excellent way to finish an autumn meal of, for example, roast hare with dark-brown cocoa sauce. See photo, p. 157.

    1/4 batch bisquit, see Chocolate bisquit, p. 98

Hot whisked meringue
    1.1 oz (30 g) egg white (about 1 white)
    2.1 oz (60 g) confectioners' sugar
    1 tsp lemon juice

Black currant mousse
    2.6 oz (75 g) black currant purée with 10% sugar (about
        4.4 oz black currants)
    1 sheet gelatin (2 g)
    1.9 oz (55 g) hot-whisked meringue
    4.4 oz (125 g) whipped cream (2/3 cup)

White chocolate mousse
    1.8 oz (50 g) white chocolate
    0.5 oz (15 g) unsalted butter
    1 tsp (5 g) white rum
    1.2 oz (35 g) hot whisked meringue
    3.9 oz (110 g) heavy cream (1/2 cup)

For decoration
    2.6 oz (75 g) white chocolate (Valrhona Ivoire, Lindt,
        Callebaut or Fazer)
    1.8 oz (50 g) semisweet chocolate (Valrhona Caraque 56%
        or Marabou dark)
    2 sheets acetate film

Gravenstein sauce

7 oz (200 g) apple
1/2 cup French apple cider from Normandy
1.4 oz (40 g) sugar

1 1/2 tbs (25 g) lemon juice
1 1/2 tbs (25 g) Calvados

1. Make Chocolate bisquit batter, pipe out 8 bases and bake, according to the recipe on p. 98. Leave to cool.

Hot-whisked meringue

2. Pour egg white, confectioners' sugar and lemon juice into a metal bowl. Whisk lightly until well mixed.
3. Place the bowl over a saucepan of simmering water. Whisk vigorously until the meringue reaches 120–140°F.
4. Continue whisking with an electric mixer at low speed, or slowly by hand, until cool.

Black currant mousse

5. Using a blender or food processor, mix the black currants to purée. Pass through a fine sieve.
6. Weigh 2.3 oz (65 g) purée and mix with 0.4 oz (10 g) sugar until dissolved.
7. Soak the gelatin sheet in plenty of cold water for about 10 minutes.
8. Whip the cream.
9. Drain the gelatin and mix into the purée, in a small saucepan. Heat up, stirring continuously, until the gelatin has dissolved and the purée is about 105°F.
10. Mix the purée into 1.9 oz (55 g) of the cooled meringue. Whisk until smooth.
11. Fold the mixture into the whipped cream.

White chocolate mousse

12. Melt the finely chopped chocolate, in a microwave oven or double boiler, to 122°F. White chocolate is easily ruined if heated for too long.
13. Stir in the butter until melted, then add the rum.
14. Stir in the remaining meringue and mix until smooth.
15. Whip the cream. Fold in the chocolate mixture and stir with a baking spatula, to a light and porous mousse.

For decoration

16. Temper the white chocolate; see p. 35. Spread out thinly, using a spatula, and cover with a sheet of acetate film. Placing a weight on the film, leave to harden.
17. Spread the remaining white chocolate on a marble slab, or other cold surface, as thinly as possible. Using a cookie cutter, make curled chocolate shavings (see chocolate techniques, p. 34–41).
18. Freeze a metal tray for at least 30 minutes. Melt the semi-sweet chocolate but do not temper. Pour into a paper cone and cut a small hole at the tip.
19. Remove the tray from the freezer and pipe out parallel threads of chocolate. Carefully loosen with a spatula and store them in the refrigerator until needed.

Gravenstein sauce

20. Peel, core and cube the apples. Pour cider, sugar and lemon juice into a saucepan.
21. Add the apple cubes and boil for about 5 minutes until softened.
22. Mix to a purée, in a blender or food processor, and add the Calvados.
23. Cover with plastic wrap and store in the refrigerator.

Assembly

24. Cut out 4 strips of acetate film, 2 inch wide and 8 1/2 inch long. Form into rings, stapling the ends together and place on parchment paper.
25. Put a bisquit base in each ring, placing the rings on parchment paper.
26. Half fill the rings of film with black currant mousse, and put the second layer of bisquit on the mousse.
27. Top up the rings with white mousse and smooth off with a spatula.
28. Freeze for at least 1 hour.
29. Take out from the freezer and remove the rings of film. Transfer the mousses to a plate each.
30. Loosen the acetate film from the chocolate. Break off tiles of chocolate and place round the edge of the mousse. Decorate with chocolate shavings and threads; see p. 157. Pour apple-sauce around each mousse.

Passion Fruit and Chocolate Bavaroise, encased with white
chocolate and topped with fresh fruit, p. 154.

Autumn Dessert, p. 154.

Japonaise Cake   12 portions

• •

This irresistible Swiss cake really explodes with hazelnuts. Preferably use Spanish almonds and Spanish or Italian hazelnuts. They have a more powerful taste than Californian almonds or Turkish hazelnuts.

   The cake will keep fresh for 3 days in the refrigerator and should be chilled when served.

Draw four 9 1/2 inch diameter circles, two on a piece each of parchment paper. Place the papers on baking sheets.

Japonaise meringue

   2.1 oz (60 g) hazelnuts
   2.1 oz (60 g) granulated sugar
   7.4 oz (210 g) egg white (about 7 whites)
   1 tsp lemon juice
   3.2 oz (90 g) granulated sugar
   1 1/2 tbs (25 g) milk, 3% fat

Praline cream

   7 oz (200 g) almonds
   7 oz (200 g) hazelnuts
   1 vanilla pod
   14 oz (400 g) sugar
   3.5 oz (100 g) water (1/2 cup)
   5.3 oz (150 g) bittersweet chocolate (Valrhona Grand Cru
      Guanaja 70.5% or Marabou dark)
   10.5 oz (300 g) unsalted butter

For decoration

   2.5 oz (70 g) bittersweet chocolate (Valrhona Grand Cru
      Guanaja 70.5% or Marabou dark)

Japonaise meringue

1. Preheat oven to 225°F.
2. Using a blender or food processor, mix the hazelnuts and sugar to a fine powder (so-called TPT).
3. In a clean stainless steel bowl, whisk together the egg white, lemon juice and 1/3 of the sugar.
4. Add the remaining sugar, stirring continuously. Whisk until stiff.
5. Mix the milk and nut powder to a firm paste.
6. Fold the nut paste into the egg white and mix until light and porous.
7. Spread or pipe (using a smooth no. 12 tip) the meringue batter equally, as smoothly as possible, into the four circles on the two pieces of parchment paper.
8. Bake for about 2 hours until golden brown, or until the meringue feels dry.

Praline cream

9. Preheat oven to 400°F.
10. Spread the almonds on a baking sheet and roast until golden.
11. Spread the hazelnuts on a baking sheet and roast until golden. Rub the hazelnuts in a tea towel to remove skins.
12. Split the vanilla pod and place in a 3-quart saucepan.
13. Add water and sugar. Heat up and boil for 5 minutes.
14. Add the almonds and hazelnuts and boil vigorously, stirring all the time, until the nuts begin to sputter and pop. Stir vigorously until the sugar begins to whiten (die). Continue to stir until sugar has melted completely and is golden brown. Pour out onto parchment paper and leave to cool.
15. Using a blender or food processor, mix to a smooth, oily liquid paste. The paste should be 158°F, to ensure that the sugar has melted completely.
16. Transfer the paste to a metal bowl. Add the chocolate, finely chopped, and stir until completely melted. Leave to stiffen, for at least 1 hour, in the refrigerator.
17. Add 10.5 oz (300 g) cold butter. Whisk at a low speed for about 15 minutes to a light, porous cream.

Assembling the cake

18. Place one meringue base on a plate and spread with 1/2 the cream. Place the next meringue on top and spread with the remaining cream. Top with the third meringue, smooth side up. Even the cake by gently pressing with a baking sheet.
19. Refrigerate until stiff.
20. Using a rolling pin, crumble the fourth meringue.
21. Carefully lift the cake, and completely cover with the crumbled meringue, spreading with a spatula.
22. Roll gently with a rolling pin to ensure that the crumbs stay in place.
23. Melt and temper the bittersweet chocolate; see p. 35. Pipe a circle of chocolate in the middle of the cake.

Tip

If you want the hazelnut flavor to be even more pronounced you can replace the chocolate in the cream with cocoa powder. By the way, did you know that the melting point of cocoa powder is 95°F, which makes it melt deliciously in your mouth.

Poire Honold Cake   12 portions

● ●

This cake is a specialty of Confiserie Honold, in Zurich. It was always incredibly popular when I worked there. It still can be found on the menu at Konditori Hollandia in Malmö after 30 years, which proves the durability of this recipe.

The cake has a delightful combination of cinnamon, chocolate, pears and raspberry.

1 adjustable cake ring, 9 inch diameter, for the pastry base
1 cake ring, 9 1/2 inch diameter, for the chocolate base

Chocolate base

0.4 oz (10 g) unsalted butter, for greasing
3 oz (85 g) all-purpose flour
1.4 oz (40 g) cocoa powder, preferably Valrhona
1.8 oz (50 g) finely ground hazelnuts
4.2 oz (120 g) egg yolk (about 6 yolks)
3 oz (85 g) sugar
4.2 oz (120 g) egg whites (about 4 whites)
3 oz (85 g) sugar

Cinnamon base

1.8 oz (50 g) unsalted butter, room temperature
0.9 oz (25 g) confectioners' sugar
1 pinch salt
0.7 oz (20 g) egg yolk (about 1 yolk)
0.9 oz (25 g) ground un-blanched almond
2.5 oz (70 g) all-purpose flour
grated zest of 1/4 lemon

Vanilla boiled Williams pears

1 vanilla pod
17.5 oz (500 g) water (2 cups)
6.1 oz (175 g) sugar
4 medium-sized ripe pears, preferably Williams (Bartlett)
1 lemon

Chocolate mousse

3.2 oz (90 g) egg white (about 3 whites)
3.2 oz (90 g) sugar
1 tsp lemon juice
4.9 oz (140 g) bittersweet chocolate (Valrhona Grand Cru Manjari 66.5% or Marabou dark)
3 tbs (50 g) milk, 3% fat
8.8 oz (250 g) heavy cream (1 cup)
3 tbs (50 g) raspberry jam, see recipe p. 89, or use bought quality jam

Chocolate shavings

4.9 oz (140 g) milk chocolate (Valrhona Jivara Lactée 40% or Marabou milk)

10.5 oz (300 g) heavy cream (1 1/4 cups)
0.7 oz (20 g) sugar

Chocolate base

1. Preheat oven to 400°F. Grease the 9 1/2 inch cake ring with 0.4 oz (10 g) unsalted butter.
2. Sift together the flour and cocoa.
3. Using a blender or food processor, pulverize the hazelnuts and add to the flour.
4. Using an electric mixer, whisk the egg yolk and sugar for 5 minutes until frothy.
5. Pour the egg white into a stainless steel bowl. Add 1/3 of the sugar and whisk lightly until stiff. Add the remaining sugar and whisk until stiff. Fold in the egg yolk froth, flour, cocoa and hazelnuts and stir to a porous batter.
6. Pour the batter in the cake ring, ensuring that it comes well up the edges. This will give a more even cake base.
7. Bake for 25–30 minutes. Use a cake tester to check that the inside of the cake is dry.
8. Take out and sprinkle with sugar. Turn upside down and leave to cool on a rack.

Cinnamon base

9. Mix the butter with sugar, grated lemon zest, salt and cinnamon. Add egg yolk.
10. Add the flour and finely ground almonds and work into dough.
11. Put the dough into a plastic bag and refrigerate for at least 30 minutes.
12. Preheat oven to 400°F.
13. Lightly flour a rolling pin, and roll out the dough to a 9 inch diameter circle.
14. Transfer the circle of dough to a parchment-covered baking sheet.
15. Prick the dough to prevent "blistering."
16. Transfer the dough to the adjustable cake ring, trimming the edges if necessary.
17. Bake for 10 minutes until golden brown. Leave to cool.

Vanilla-boiled pears

18. Split the vanilla pod.
19. Pour the water and sugar into a 2-quart saucepan. Add the vanilla pod and bring to a boil.
20. Peel the pears, quarter and remove the cores. Place in a saucepan.
21. Divide the lemon. Squeeze the juice over the pears.
22. Simmer until soft. Remove from the heat and cool so that the pears do not get too soft.

(This can be done a day in advance.)

Chocolate mousse

23. Mix the egg white, sugar and lemon juice in a metal bowl. Place the bowl in a saucepan of simmering water. Whisk with an electric mixer until 130–140°F. Transfer the bowl to a saucepan of cold water and continue to whisk, at a low speed, until the mixture has cooled.
24. Finely chop the chocolate and melt. Add the milk and heat to 110–120°F, stirring continuously.
25. Whip the cream until it forms soft tops.
26. Stir together the chocolate-milk and egg mixture into a smooth cream. Fold in the whipped cream.

Assembling the cake

27. Place the cinnamon base in the 9 1/2 inch baking ring. Spread with raspberry jam, using a spatula.
28. Divide the chocolate base into 2 equally thick layers. Place one layer on the jam and press gently. Freeze the other layer for a later occasion.
29. Drain the pears in a colander and arrange over the chocolate base.
30. Cover with chocolate mousse and smooth with a spatula. Tap the cake twice on the table to even it out.
31. Cover with plastic wrap and freeze for at least 2 hours.

Chocolate shavings

32. Finely chop the chocolate and heat in a microwave oven to 110–120°F.
33. Spread the chocolate thinly over a marble slab or draining board. Leave to harden.
34. Scrape chocolate shavings, using the point of a knife, see photo, p. 41.
35. Whisk the cream and sugar until stiffened.
36. Remove the frozen cake from the baking ring and cover with the whipped cream. Cover with chocolate shavings and defrost in a refrigerator.

The hot-whisked meringue gives the chocolate mousse a different character, which is well suited to this cake.

Delicious with pear cognac, or Eau de Vie au Poire Williams.

Tip
Well wrapped, this cake can keep for weeks in the freezer. Defrost for about 1 hour before serving.

Chocolate Meringue Swiss   12 portions

• •

This cake is known as Vacherin in Switzerland and France. When I began my career in the early 1960s, every Swedish bakery used to make meringue Swiss, with special boxes for safe transport home.

It consists of light meringue with whipped cream and powerfully flavored chocolate cream. Meringue Swiss should have a powerful chocolate taste, and here I have chosen Guanaja.

Draw three 9 inch diameter circles on a sheet of parchment paper

Meringue
4.2 oz (120 g) egg white (about 4 whites)
1 tsp lemon juice
8.4 oz (240 g) sugar

For decoration and coating the bases
4.9 oz (140 g) bittersweet chocolate (Valrhona Grand Cru Guanaja 70.5% or Marabou dark)

For assembly

28 oz (800 g) heavy cream (3 1/4 cups)

1.1 oz (30 g) sugar

4.9 oz (140 g) bittersweet chocolate (Valrhona Grand Cru
Guanaja 70.5% or Marabou dark)

2 tbs (30 g) milk, 3% fat

Meringue

1. Preheat oven to 275°F.
2. Half fill a 5-quart saucepan with water and boil.
3. Whisk together egg white, lemon juice and sugar in a metal
   bowl. Place the bowl in a saucepan of simmering water and
   whisk until 130–140°C, using an electric mixer.
4. Remove the bowl and whisk until cool at medium speed, or
   by hand using a balloon whisk.
5. Using a pastry bag with a smooth or fluted tip, pipe a thick
   circle of meringue. Then pipe a thick cross over the circle,
   see photo below.
6. Place the baking sheet with meringues in the oven and
   lower the heat to 210°F. Leave to dry for about 2 hours.
   (The meringues can be made several days in advance and
   stored dry.)

For decoration and coating

7. Melt and temper the chocolate; see p. 35.
8. Using a soft brush dipped in chocolate, coat the meringues.
9. Use the remaining chocolate to make a chocolate latticework
   roll; see p. 40.
10. Harden the roll in the refrigerator. Remove the film, and
    carefully break into 2 equal pieces.

Assembly

11. Whip the cream and sugar until it begins to stiffen.
    Refrigerate.
12. Pour the milk into a microwave bowl and add the finely
    chopped chocolate. Melt the chocolate, stirring continuously,
    and bring the mixture to 140°F.
13. Fold the chocolate sauce into half the whipped cream. Blend
    to a smooth chocolate cream.
14. Place a meringue base on a glass cake stand. Fill one half
    with a 1 inch layer of plain cream. Fill the other half with
    chocolate cream.
15. Place the next meringue on top and repeat the filling proce-
    dure, letting the plain cream and chocolate cream switch
    place. Place the third meringue on top.
16. Using a pastry bag with a no. 12 fluted tip, pipe chocolate
    cream over one half of the cake and plain cream over the
    other.
17. Decorate with the chocolate rolls. Keep in a refrigerator until
    time for serving

Use a smooth tip to pipe the meringue.

CHAPTER 9

ice cream bombs and ice cream cakes

Bombe Parma   6–8 portions

• •

When I first started to work at a restaurant, we would serve ice cream bombs on special occasions. This beautiful, eye-catching dessert is a guaranteed success at a New Year or other party. Valrhona Grand Cru Manjari chocolate, with its tangy criollo bean flavor, combines perfectly with the orange-flavored filling.

1-quart, half sphere mold

Chocolate meringue base
1.1 oz (30 g) egg white (about 1 white)
1 drop freshly squeezed lemon juice
1.1 oz (30 g) sugar
1.1 oz (30 g) confectioners' sugar
1 tsp (6 g) cocoa powder

Parfait filling
2.1 oz (60 g) water (1/4 cup)
5.3 oz (150 g) sugar
4.2 oz (120 g) egg yolk (about 6 yolks)
14 oz (400 g) heavy cream (1 3/4 cups)
2 oranges
3.5 oz (100 g) bittersweet chocolate (Valrhona Grand Cru Manjari 64.5% or Marabou dark)

1 batch chocolate glaze; see Othello p. 132

For latticework chocolate roll; see p. 38
3.5 oz (100 g) bittersweet chocolate (Valrhona Grand Cru Manjari 64.5% or Marabou dark)
1 sheet acetate film

For decorative marbled discs; see p. 42
1.8 oz (50 g) white chocolate (Valrhona Ivoire, Lindt, Fazer or Callebaut)
1 sheet acetate film
1.8 oz (50 g) semisweet chocolate (Valrhona Caraque 56% or Marabou dark)

Chocolate meringue base
1. Preheat oven to 275°F.
2. Whisk the chilled egg white and lemon juice until the foam begins to lift.
3. Sprinkle in 1.1 oz (30 g) sugar. With an electric mixer at medium speed or by hand, mix until stiff.
4. Finely sift the cocoa and confectioners' sugar directly into the bowl. Fold into the meringue mixture, using a baking spatula.

5. Draw a 6 1/2 inch diameter circle on parchment paper.
6. Using a pastry bag with a smooth no. 10 tip, pipe the meringue into the circle. Smooth out with a spatula.
7. Bake for 30 minutes, ensuring that the meringue is still soft in the middle.
8. Leave to cool on a rack.

Parfait style filling
(known as pâté à bombe in French kitchens)
9. Measure the water into a small 1-quart saucepan. Add sugar and stir with a whisk until the sugar has dissolved.
10. Bring to the boil and skim.
11. Use a brush dipped in cold water to wash down any sugar crystals that may form on the sides of the pan. Bring the sugar syrup to 225°F.
12. Whisk the egg yolks, by hand or using an electric mixer, to a firm froth.
13. Boil the sugar syrup vigorously to 252°F, use a thermometer or do a ball test; see p. 44.
14. Stirring continuously, whisk the boiling syrup into the egg yolk froth.
15. Whisk at low speed until the mixture has cooled, and place in the refrigerator.
16. Whip the cream, not too firm, and refrigerate.
17. Thoroughly wash the oranges. Grate off the zests, using a fine grater.
18. Squeeze out the juice and pour into a small saucepan. Boil until 1 tablespoon of syrupy juice remains.
19. Pour this juice over the grated zests and massage with a spatula until all the essential oils have been released from the zests.
20. Finely chop the chocolate. Melt in a microwave oven or double boiler to 130°F.
21. Remove the chilled egg yolk mixture from the refrigerator.
22. Fold in the whipped cream, using a baking spatula.
23. Divide the mixture into 2 bowls. Add the orange zests to one of them.
24. Stir half the mixture without orange into the melted chocolate, and mix until smooth. Then add the remaining half.
25. Pour the chocolate parfait into the half sphere mold.
26. Fill a pastry bag with the orange parfait. Insert the tip into the chocolate parfait and pipe out the orange parfait. Continue until the mold is full, with the chocolate parfait on the outside.
27. Loosen the meringue base from the parchment paper and place it over the parfait. Press down gently.
28. Freeze for at least 6 hours before eating, or prepare the previous day.
29. Make the chocolate decorations; see pp. 38 and 42. This can be done several days in advance, to avoid stress.

30. Make a batch of chocolate glaze, see Othello recipe on p. 132. Heat to 95°F in a microwave oven or double boiler, while stirring.
31. Remove the bomb from the freezer and dip the mold in lukewarm water.
32. Carefully dry the bottom of the mold with a tea towel.
33. Unmold the bomb by pressing one side of the mold and twirling.
34. Place the ice cream bomb on a somewhat smaller baking pan (see photo).
35. Pour the glaze over the ice cream and allow to drip off. Smooth the underside with a spatula and carefully move the bomb to a cake stand.
36. Decorate with marbled chocolate tiles around the bomb and the latticework rolls on top.
37. Defrost for about 30 minutes in the refrigerator.

Tip

The ice cream bomb can be made several days in advance. The meringue base not only tastes good but also prevents the ice cream sliding around the plate when serving.

Coupe Belle Helène   12 portions

• •

This classic combination of pear/vanilla ice cream and chocolate sauce was created by Auguste Escoffier, the king of chefs. Since then, Coupe Belle Helène has been a classic dessert the world over. The combination of pear and chocolate has many fans, old and new.

   1999 vintage Gran Couva, with 68% cocoa beans from Trinidad, was quite fantastic and took chocolate ice cream to new heights. Let's hope following vintages will continue this trend!

Chocolate bases (2)

1.4 oz (40 g) almonds
2.8 oz (80 g) sugar
4.2 oz (120 g) bittersweet chocolate (Valrhona Grand Cru
     Pur Caraïbe 66.5% or Marabou dark)
4.2 oz (120 g) unsalted butter, room temperature
2.8 oz (80 g) egg yolk (about 4 yolks)
1.1 oz (30 g) all-purpose flour
4.2 oz (120 g) egg white (about 4 whites)
1 tsp freshly squeezed lemon juice
2.8 oz (80 g) sugar

Gran Couva chocolate ice cream

1 sheet gelatin (2 g)
1 vanilla pod
8.8 oz (250 g) heavy cream (1 cup)
8.8 oz (250 g) milk (1 cup)
0.9 oz (25 g) honey
4.2 oz (120 g) egg yolk (about 6 yolks)
4.4 oz (125 g) raw sugar
5.3 oz (150 g) bittersweet chocolate (Valrhona Gran Couva
68% or Marabou dark)

Pear ice cream

17.5 oz (500 g) ripe, cored and peeled pears, preferably
     Williams (Bartlett)
3 tbs freshly squeezed lemon juice
3.5 oz (100 g) sugar
1 sheet gelatin (2 g)
1 vanilla pod
3.5 oz (100 g) heavy cream (1/2 cup)
0.9 oz (25 g) honey
1.4 oz (40 g) egg yolk (about 2 yolks)
1.8 oz (50 g) sugar
3 tbs Eau de Vie Poire Williams

5.3 oz (150 g) bittersweet chocolate (Valrhona Gran Couva
     68% or Marabou dark)
1.8 oz (50 g) white chocolate (Valrhona Ivoire, see
     marbling)

1 beautiful, ripe pear for decoration

Caramel glaze

1.8 oz (50 g) water (1/4 cup)
3.5 oz (100 g) sugar
1 tsp white wine vinegar

1/2 batch chocolate glaze; see Othello p. 132

DAY 1

Make 2 chocolate bases

1. Draw 2 circles, 9 and 9 1/2 inch diameter respectively, on a sheet of parchment paper. Preheat oven to 350°F.
2. In a blender or food processor, powder the un-blanched almonds and sugar.
3. Finely chop the chocolate. Melt carefully in a microwave oven or a double boiler and heat to 113°F.
4. Whisk the butter into the chocolate. When the butter has melted, whisk in the egg yolk and almond-sugar powder.
5. Sieve the flour onto a plate or paper.
6. Whisk together the egg white, lemon juice and sugar.
7. Fold the chocolate sauce into the meringue mixture, using a baking spatula. Mix until light and porous. Fold in the flour.
8. Spread out, or pipe, the cake bases in the circles. Bake for about 12 minutes until the cakes feels firm but still somewhat soft. Leave to cool on racks. Cover with plastic wrap and store in the freezer until the following day.

Gran Couva chocolate ice cream

9. Soak the gelatin in cold water for about 10 minutes.
10. Split the vanilla pod and scrape out the seeds into a saucepan. Add the cream, milk and honey and bring to the boil.
11. Beat the egg yolk and raw sugar until fluffy.
12. Pour the cream mixture into the egg froth and whisk thoroughly.
13. Return to the saucepan and bring to 185°F, stirring continuously. Do a rose or spoon test (see p. 45) if you do not have a thermometer.
14. Drain the gelatin sheet and melt into the hot cream. Add the chopped chocolate and stir until melted.
15. Pour the chocolate cream through a fine sieve. Cool the cream quickly in a saucepan of cold water. Cover with plastic and refrigerate overnight, or preferably 24 hours.

Pear ice cream

16. Peel and cut the ripe pears into pieces. Place in a microwave bowl or saucepan and pour over the freshly squeezed lemon juice. Mix in the sugar, and boil until the pears are quite soft. Preferably use a microwave oven for a nicer color.
17. Soak the gelatin in cold water for about 10 minutes.
18. In a blender or food processor, mix the pears into a smooth purée. Pass the purée through a fine strainer.
19. Drain the gelatin sheet and melt into the hot purée. Cool quickly in a saucepan of cold water.

20. Split the vanilla pod and scrape the seeds into a saucepan, together with the empty pod. Add cream and honey and bring to the boil.
21. Whisk the egg yolk and sugar until frothy.
22. Pour the cream mixture into the egg froth and whisk thoroughly.

23. Return to the saucepan and bring to 185°F, stirring continuously. Do a rose or spoon test (see p. 45) if you do not have a thermometer.
24. Pour the cream through a fine strainer into the purée, and stir carefully until quite cool.
25. Flavor with pear schnapps.

Recipe continues on following page

Tip

This recipe has many steps, but everything can be prepared in advance to avoid stress. Serve with hot chocolate sauce and a glass of fine wine—this cake deserves it!

DAY 2

Assembling the cake

26. Cut 2 strips of acetate film, 1 inch wide and 30 1/2 inch long. Form into 2 rings, 9 1/2 inch diameter, stapling the ends together.
27. Pour the chocolate cream into an ice-cream maker and run for 30–45 minutes until firm. Otherwise, you can put the cream in the refrigerator, removing occasionally to stir.
28. Place one of the rings of film on a plate covered with parchment paper. Fill the ring with chocolate ice cream and freeze for at least 4 hours.
29. Repeat the procedure with pear ice cream. The ice cream can be kept in the freezer for 2 weeks, if you wish to do your preparations early.

(You can prepare the cake as far as this in advance.)

30. Melt and temper the chocolate; see p. 35. Spread the chocolate thinly on a sheet of acetate film; use for making chocolate tiles. Make a spiral with the remaining chocolate; see p. 38.
31. <u>Glaze the pear:</u> Measure the water into a small saucepan and add the sugar, whisking continuously. Simmer until the sugar has completely dissolved. Skim if necessary. Add the vinegar and then boil vigorously. Keep brushing the syrup down from the sides of the pan to prevent crystallization. When the caramel is light yellow, pour it evenly over the pear, placed on a rack. Leave the pear to cool on parchment paper.

Serving

32. Place the 9 inch cake base on a cake stand. Removing the outer film, place the chocolate ice cream on the cake base. Remove the film, and place the pear ice cream on top.
33. Place the 9 1/2 inch cake base on top and gently press in place.
34. Heat the chocolate glaze to 95°F, in a microwave oven or double boiler, stirring often. Pour the glaze over the cake and spread evenly with a spatula.
35. Decorate the edge of the cake with chocolate tiles.
36. Finally, decorate with the glazed pear and chocolate spiral.

Tip

You can make milk chocolate glaze in the following way:

8.8 oz (250 g) milk, 3% fat
3.5 oz (100 g) honey
4 sheets of gelatin
10.5 oz (300 g) milk chocolate (Jivara Lactée or Marabou milk)
10.5 oz (300 g) apricot jam, neutral

Soak the gelatin in plenty of cold water for at least 10 minutes. Make a ganache of milk, honey and milk chocolate. Drain the gelatin and melt into the ganache. Add the apricot jam and blend until smooth. Use this as a chocolate glaze.

Apricot jam
35 oz (1000 g) pitted apricots
26.5 oz (750 g) sugar
juice of 2 lemons
4 bitter almonds

1. *Mix the ingredients in a 4-quart saucepan and marinate for 24 hours.*
2. *Bring to the boil, stirring constantly. Skim the surface.*
3. *Using a hand blender, mix until smooth. Pass through a strainer and return to the saucepan. Boil to 220–225°F.*

Left: Belle Helène, p. 168. Right: A face of semisweet chocolate (from a gelatin mold created by the author), with a small cherub made of white chocolate below.

Coconut Parfait with Flambéed Pineapple
serves 4

4 round coffee cups or similar individual molds

2.8 oz (80 g) bittersweet chocolate (Valrhona Grand Cru Guanaja 70.5% or Marabou dark)

Parfait
3.5 oz (100 g) coconut milk
2.8 oz (80 g) white chocolate (Valrhona Ivoire, Lindt or Callebaut)
0.4 oz (10 g) white rum
3.5 oz (100 g) heavy cream
0.5 oz (15 g) freshly squeezed lime juice
0.9 oz (25 g) lemongrass
28 oz (800 g) pineapple, Del Monte extra sweet

Sauce
2.8 oz (80 g) light raw sugar, cassonade or muscovardo
1.8 oz (50 g) dark rum, preferably Captain Morgan
0.9 oz (25 g) brown cocoa liqueur, Marie Brizard
0.4 oz (10 g) black pepper
1.8 oz (50 g) unsalted butter

1. Place the cups or containers in the freezer. Melt the finely chopped chocolate in a microwave oven or double boiler, stirring often, and bring to 104°F.
2. Brush the insides of the cups with the chocolate, using a pastry brush. Return to the freezer and repeat the procedure until all the chocolate has been used. Finely chop the white chocolate. Finely chop and crush the lemon grass. Squeeze out the lime juice. Add both to the coconut milk and bring to the boil. Leave to set for 10 minutes. Bring back to the boil and pour over the chopped chocolate. Using a hand blender or electric mixer, blend to a smooth ganache. Cover with plastic wrap and leave to cool for 60 minutes, at room temperature. Whip the cream until light and fluffy. Fold into the ganache, together with rum, and mix with a baking spatula to a light, porous parfait.
3. Fill the cups with parfait and place in the freezer for 30 minutes. Remove from the freezer and press the parfait up the sides, using a spoon dipped in hot water, to make a hollow in the middle of the "coconut." Replace in the freezer and freeze for at least 3 hours, preferably overnight. (Can be kept for several days in the freezer if wrapped in plastic.)
4. Remove the outer skin, and cut the pineapple into 8 slices, 1/2 inch thick. Remove the core.
5. Sprinkle with ground pepper.
6. Brown the butter in a flambé pan and brown the pineapple slices, 4 at a time. Remove the slices and put to one side.
7. Remove the parfait from the cups and place on 4 plates. Decorate with some pineapple leaves.
8. In the flambé pan, stir some sugar into the butter and heat until it begins to caramelize. Add the pineapple slices and reheat. Pour over cocoa liqueur and bring to the boil.
9. Flambé with rum, shaking the pan to ensure that it burns evenly.
10. Arrange the pineapple slices on the plates and pour the liqueur sauce over them. Serve immediately.

Tip

Remember to take out the parfait in good time. It should be soft when served. Make sure the pineapple slices are really hot when you flambé them or the rum will not burn.

CHAPTER 10

mousses, brûlées, and bavaroises

Crème Brûlée—with pistachios, chocolate, wild strawberries, and cocoa nougatine

4 portions

• • •

This kind of brûlée contains gelatin and is known by professionals as molded brûlé. The gelatin makes it possible to use two different kinds of brûlé at the same time. Chocolate brûlée, however, needs no gelatin since the chocolate will harden anyway.

Pistachio brûlée
1 sheet gelatin
5.3 oz (150 g) heavy cream (3/4 cup)
1.8 oz (50 g) milk (1/4 cup)
2.8 oz (80 g) egg yolk (about 4 yolks)
1.4 oz (40 g) sugar
1.2 oz (35 g) pistachios
orange-flower water, can be found at herb stores or
      delicatessens

Chocolate brûlée
2.8 oz (80 g) bittersweet chocolate (Valrhona Grand Cru
      Manjari 64.5% or Marabou dark)
4.4 oz (125 g) heavy cream (2/3 cup)
1.4 oz (40 g) egg yolk (about 2 yolks)
0.7 oz (20 g) raw sugar
1.8 oz (50 g) cassonade or sugar cane
7 oz (200 g) fresh wild strawberries, or other red berries

Cocoa and coffee nougatine
2.6 oz (75 g) sugar
1 pinch pectin
0.4 oz (12 g) honey
2.1 oz (60 g) unsalted butter
2.1 oz (60 g) skinned and crushed cocoa beans, can be
      bought at herb stores
0.7 oz (20 g) crushed coffee beans, preferably Pur Arabica

Pistachio brûlée
1. Soak the gelatin in cold water for about 10 minutes.
2. Boil together the cream and milk.
3. Whisk the egg yolk and sugar until light and fluffy.
4. Pour the hot cream-milk into the egg froth. Mix well.
5. Pour the mixture into a saucepan. Stirring with a wooden spoon, carefully heat until the mixture begins to thicken, at 185°F. Do a rose or spoon test (see p. 45) if you do not have a thermometer.

6. Pass the cream through a fine strainer.
7. Drain the gelatin sheet.
8. Stir the gelatin into the hot cream until completely melted.
9. Crush the pistachios, with a drop of orange-flower water, in a mortar. Mix to a fine paste.
10. Scrape the pistachio paste and 3/4 cup of the brûlée cream into a blender or food processor. Mix until completely smooth.
11. Scrape the pistachio cream back into the saucepan with the remaining brûlée cream and mix thoroughly.
12. Half fill 4 low, ovenproof dishes with the brûlée and leave to stiffen in the freezer, about 20 minutes.

Chocolate brûlée
13. Finely chop the chocolate.
14. Boil the cream. Whisk the egg and sugar until fluffy and light.
15. Pour the hot cream into the egg froth. Mix well.
16. Pour the mixture into a saucepan. Stirring with a wooden spoon, carefully heat the mixture until it begins to thicken, at 185°F. Do a rose or spoon test (see p. 45) if you do not have a thermometer.
17. Add the chopped chocolate and stir until melted. Pass the cream through a fine strainer.
18. Pour the chocolate brûlée over the pistachio brûlée and refrigerate the dishes, covered with plastic wrap.

Cocoa and coffee nougatine
19. Preheat oven to 350°F.
20. Mix sugar and pectin.
21. Boil up the honey with the butter. Add the pectin-sugar and boil until the mixture begins to come away from the sides of the saucepan. Add the crushed beans and mix thoroughly.
22. Quickly spread the paste on a baking sheet covered with a baking cloth or silpat.
23. Bake for 15–17 minutes. It's better to bake for a shorter time to prevent the nougatine becoming too chewy.

(You can prepare as far as this in advance.)

Storage
Will keep for 2 weeks in an airtight container.

24. Set the oven to "grill."
25. Sift the dishes with sugar. Place them near the grill or use a blow torch. Gratinate until the sugar has caramelized. Leave to cool.
26. Break off irregular pieces of nougatine and stick into the brûlée. Decorate with wild strawberries.

Tip

Orange-flower water

is used to draw out

and heighten the flavor

of the pistachios.

White Chocolate Bavaroise—with rhubarb slivers and berries 6–8 portions

• •

1 baking pan (the photo shows a charlotte mold)

Rhubarb slivers
about 3/4 lb rhubarb
confectioners' sugar
175°F oven

Raspberry and currant gel
1 1/2 gelatin sheets
1.8 oz (50 g) sugar
1.8 oz (50 g) water (1/4 cup)
3.5 oz (100 g) raspberries
1.8 oz (50 g) red currants

Hazelnut praline powder
0.9 oz (25 g) roasted and skinned hazelnuts
0.7 oz (20 g) sugar
2 tsp water (10 g)

Bavaroise
3 gelatin sheets
1 vanilla pod, preferably Tahitian
8.8 oz (250 g) milk (1 cup)
2.8 oz (80 g) egg yolk (about 4 yolks)
2.8 oz (80 g) sugar
7 oz (200 g) white chocolate (Valrhona Ivoire, Lindt or
    Callebaut)
1/4 cup Cointreau
8 oz (225 g) whipped cream (7/8 cup)
1.6 oz (45 g) hazelnut praline powder

Decoration
7 oz (200 g) fresh raspberries
3.5 oz (100 g) red currants
confectioners' sugar

Rhubarb slivers
1. Preheat oven to 175°F.
2. Cut the rhubarb into pieces, the same length as the height of the baking tin.
3. Using a cheese slice or slicing machine, make as thin slivers as possible. Place them on a baking cloth and powder with confectioners' sugar.
4. Leave for 2–3 hours, until completely dry.

Hazelnut praline powder
5. Preheat oven to 400°F.
6. Spread the hazelnuts over a baking sheet and roast for about 10 minutes, stirring often.
7. Rub off the skins, using a tea towel.
8. Boil the sugar and water until it begins to turn yellow.
9. Add the nuts and caramelize them, stirring constantly, until golden yellow.
10. Pour out onto parchment paper and leave to cool. Crush in a mortar.

Raspberry and currant gel
11. Soak the gelatin for 10 minutes in cold water.
12. Boil the sugar and water in a small saucepan.
13. Remove from the heat.
14. Drain the gelatin sheets.
15. Put the gelatin sheets in the sugar syrup and stir until melted.
16. Stir in the berries and mix thoroughly.
17. Pour the gel into a teacup and leave to stiffen in the freezer for about 30 minutes.

White chocolate bavaroise
18. Soak the gelatin in cold water for 10 minutes. Split the vanilla pod. Scrape the seeds into a saucepan of milk, and add the vanilla pod.
19. Bring to a boil. Remove from the heat and leave to draw for 10–15 minutes.
20. Whisk the egg yolk and sugar until light and fluffy.
21. Remove the vanilla pod from the saucepan and pour the hot milk into the egg froth. Mix thoroughly.
22. Return the mixture to the saucepan. Stirring constantly with a wooden spoon, heat carefully until it begins to thicken, at 185°F. Do a rose or spoon test; see p. 45, if you do not have a thermometer.
23. Pour the mixture through a fine strainer.
24. Remove the gelatin sheet from the water. Without draining, immediately add to the hot mixture.
25. Stir carefully until the gelatin has dissolved.
26. Finely chop the chocolate and melt it in the mixture.

27. Add the Cointreau and cool to 65°F, over a saucepan of cold water.
28. Lightly whip the cream. Fold the chocolate mixture, a half at a time, into the whipped cream.
29. Fold in the hazelnut praline powder.
30. Half fill the baking pan with chocolate cream and place in the freezer for 5 minutes.
31. Remove the teacup of raspberry and currant gel from the freezer. Dip the cup in lukewarm water to loosen the gel.
32. Remove the bavaroise from the freezer and press the gel into the middle. Spread the remaining bavaroise on top and leave in the freezer to stiffen for at least 3 hours.

Serving

33. Dip the baking pan in lukewarm water. Carefully dry with a tea towel. Shake the bavaroise to loosen, and place on a cake plate.
34. Decorate with fresh berries and powder with confectioners' sugar.
35. Line the edge of the cake with rhubarb slivers just before serving, so that they do not soften.

Tip

If you want to make the chocolate bavaroise with bittersweet chocolate, use 5.6 oz (160 g) chocolate but increase the amount of sugar by 1.6 oz (45 g) to sweeten the chocolate.

White Chocolate Bavaroise, with rhubarb slivers and red berries, p. 178.

Chocolate Terrine Pur Caraïbe with peppermint sauce Anglaise, p. 182.

Chocolate Terrine Pur Caraïbe with Peppermint Sauce Anglaise
8 portions

• •

I have demonstrated this delicious terrine many times. I have sometimes called it the "dietician's nightmare" due to the abundance of calories.

It's so scrumptious that even a thin slice is worth a bike ride afterwards…

Pistachio and walnut bisquit

1.8 oz (50 g) pistachios
2.6 oz (75 g) sugar
2.6 oz (75 g) almonds
1.8 oz (50 g) walnuts
1 tsp Nescafé, dark roasted
1.8 oz (50 g) egg (about 1 egg)
3.5 oz (100 g) egg yolk (about 5 yolks)
3.2 oz (90 g) cornstarch
1.8 oz (50 g) butter
3.2 oz (90 g) egg white (about 3 whites)
1 tsp lemon juice
1.2 oz (35 g) sugar

Chocolate mousse

7.4 oz (210 g) unsalted butter
3.5 oz (100 g) cocoa, preferably Valrhona
5.8 oz (165 g) bittersweet chocolate (Valrhona Grand Cru
Pur Caraïbe 66.5% or Marabou dark)
13 oz (375 g) heavy cream (1 2/3 cups)
1 vanilla pod
3.5 oz (100 g) egg yolk (about 5 yolks)
7 oz (200 g) confectioners' sugar
1.8 oz (50 g) Cointreau (1/4 cup)

Peppermint sauce Anglaise

(makes about 1 1/2 cups sauce)
1 vanilla pod
0.4 oz (10 g) fresh peppermint
8.8 oz (250 g) milk (1 cup)
2.1 oz (60 g) egg yolk (about 3 yolks)
4.4 oz (125 g) sugar

Decoration

16 striped chocolate batons; see p. 40
peppermint leaves
confectioners' sugar

Pistachio and walnut bisquit

1. Preheat oven to 425°F.
2. Blend the pistachios, sugar, almonds, walnuts and Nescafé into a fine powder.
3. Whisk the egg, egg yolk and nut powder with an electric mixer for about 10 minutes.
4. Sift the cornstarch onto a plate or paper. Melt the butter.
5. Whisk the egg white, lemon juice and sugar until stiff.
6. Fold in the egg-nut mixture, using a baking spatula. Fold in the sifted cornstarch.
7. Take a spoonful of the mixture and mix carefully with the melted butter. Pour back into the mixture and beat to a porous batter.
8. Using a spatula, spread out the batter absolutely evenly over a baking cloth or parchment paper.
9. Bake for 7–8 minutes.
10. Immediately remove the bisquit base so that it does not dry out.

Chocolate mousse

11. Boil the butter and add the sifted cocoa. Using an electric mixer, mix until smooth. Add the finely chopped chocolate and whisk until completely melted.
12. Lightly whip the cream and refrigerate. Divide the vanilla pod and scrape the seeds into the chocolate butter.
13. Whisk the egg yolk and sugar until light and fluffy. Add the Cointreau, and evenly pour the chocolate butter into the egg froth. Mix until smooth.
14. Fold the chocolate mixture into the whipped cream. Mix until smooth.
15. Line a 1-quart loaf pan with plastic film.
16. Cut out 4 bisquit bases, the same length and width as the loaf pan.
17. Place the first layer in the bottom of the pan. Pipe out 1/3 of the chocolate mixture and cover with the next bisquit layer. Repeat until the loaf pan is filled.
18. Gently press down the top layer to compress the terrine. Wrap carefully with plastic and place in the freezer.

Peppermint sauce Anglaise

19. Split the vanilla pod and scrape the seeds into a saucepan. Pour in the milk and add the chopped peppermint and vanilla pod. Bring to a boil.
20. Remove from the heat and leave to draw for 10–15 minutes. Take out the vanilla pod.
21. Whisk the egg yolk and sugar for 4–5 minutes until the mixture is thick and light.
22. Pour the hot milk over the egg mixture and stir thoroughly.

23. Pour the mixture back into the saucepan. Stirring constantly with a wooden spoon, heat carefully until the sauce begins to thicken, at about 185°F. If you do not have a thermometer, do a rose or spoon test; see p. 45.

24. Strain the sauce into a chilled bowl and cool as quickly as possible, by placing in a bowl of cold, running water. Cover with plastic wrap and refrigerate for at least 1 hour, preferably overnight.

Serving

25. Unpan the chocolate terrine. Cut into 8 slices, using a knife dipped in hot water. Dry the knife between each slice.

26. Arrange the slices on plates. Pour the peppermint sauce around the slices and decorate with chocolate batons, a sprig of peppermint leaves and confectioners' sugar.

Gran Couva Millefeuille with Milk Chocolate Mousse   4 portions

• •

The contrast between the milk chocolate and bittersweet chocolate is very refined. The mousse has a flavor reminiscent of Bailey's liqueur. Kumquat in aspic is the perfect accompaniment.

Kumquat in aspic
1/2 vanilla pod
1/2 inch cinnamon
2 anise stars
2/3 cup water
2.6 oz (75 g) sugar
12 kumquats

Whisky mousse
2.6 oz (75 g) milk chocolate (Valrhona Jivara Lactée 40% or Marabou milk)
7 oz (200 g) heavy cream (7/8 cup)
0.7 oz (20 g) quality malt whisky (1/8 cup)

2.6 oz (75 g) bittersweet chocolate (Valrhona Gran Couva 68% or Marabou dark)
2 sheets acetate film
confectioners' sugar

Kumquat in aspic

1. Split the vanilla pod and scrape the seeds into a small saucepan. Add the cinnamon, anise stars and vanilla pod.

2. Pour the sugar and water into the saucepan and boil for 5 minutes.

3. Dividing the kumquats in halves, add and boil for 5 minutes.

4. Pour into a bowl, cover with plastic wrap, allow to cool and refrigerate.

Whisky mousse

5. Finely chop the milk chocolate and place in a small bowl. Boil the cream and pour over the chocolate. Using a hand blender or electric mixer, blend until smooth.

6. Add the whisky and mix thoroughly.

7. Cool as quickly as possible, placing the bowl in a saucepan of cold, running water.

8. Cover with plastic wrap and refrigerate for at least 3 hours.

9. Temper the bittersweet chocolate; see p. 35. Spread thinly over the acetate sheet. Just before the chocolate hardens (see chocolate techniques p. 34) cut into 3 equally-sized lengths and divide each length into 4 rectangles. Cover with the other acetate sheet, place a weight on top, to prevent the chocolate curling, and place in the refrigerator to harden.

10. Make some striped chocolate batons for decoration; see p. 40.

11. Whip the chilled mousse, with an electric mixer or by hand. Do not whisk too quickly or the mousse will curdle.

12. Loosen 4 rectangles of chocolate from the acetate sheet and place on parchment paper.

13. Using a paper cone, or pastry bag with a smooth no. 10 tip, pipe out half the mousse on the chocolate rectangles.

14. Place the next rectangle on top and pipe out the remaining mousse. Cover with the third rectangle and lightly powder with confectioners' sugar. Decorate with a chocolate baton.

15. Transfer to plates and serve with the kumquat.

Millefeuille made with Valrhona Grand Couva and milk chocolate mousse.
Served with kumquat, p. 183.

Pineapple Tartar with White Malibu Chocolate Mousse   4 portions

• •

I made this delicious, light chocolate dessert for a guest appearance with Leif Mannerström at the Gondolen restaurant in Stockholm. Erik Lallerstedt and Leif are good friends and both have a keen eye for fresh ingredients and satisfied customers. I had great fun creating desserts for Leif's main dishes. See photo p. 186.

White chocolate mousse
2.6 oz (75 g) white chocolate (Valrhona Ivoire, Lindt, Callebaut or Fazer)
7 oz (200 g) heavy cream (7/8 cup)
0.7 oz (20 g) Malibu coconut liqueur (1/8 cup)

Basic sugar syrup
4.4 oz (125 g) water (2/3 cup)
6.0 oz (170 g) sugar
2 tbs glucose (30 g)
2 tbs lemon juice (30 g)

For pineapple and banana slivers
1 unripe banana
4 slices of a large, fresh 1 3/4 lb pineapple (preferably Del Monte extra sweet)

Sugar syrup with basil
1.8 oz (50 g) sugar syrup from the fruit
10 basil leaves

Chocolate fans for decoration
2.6 oz (75 g) bittersweet chocolate (Valrhona Chuao or Marabou dark); see p. 40

White chocolate mousse
1. Finely chop the chocolate and place in a bowl.
2. Boil half the cream and pour over the chocolate. Mix until smooth, using a hand blender or whisk.
3. Blend in the cold cream and liqueur. Pour into a bowl and cover with plastic wrap and refrigerate for at least 3 hours.

Sugar syrup
4. Boil together the sugar and water in a saucepan. Use a brush dipped in cold water to wash down any sugar crystals that may form on the side of the pan. Skim with a tea strainer.
5. Add the glucose and re-boil. Add the lemon juice, pour into a sterilized glass jar and seal. Sugar syrup can be kept for 2 weeks in the refrigerator.

Fruit slivers
6. Preheat oven to 175°F.
7. Cut the unripe banana into 8 wafer-thin slices. Dip them into the sugar syrup and place on parchment paper. Do not leave the banana slices in sugar syrup or they will fall to pieces.
8. Peel the pineapple carefully and cut 4 wafer-thin slices. Place the slices in sugar syrup for 30 minutes before transferring to parchment paper.
9. Dry for 4 hours in the oven.

Sugar syrup with basil
10. Using a blender or food processor, mix 1.8 oz (50 g) sugar syrup (from the fruit slivers) with 10 basil leaves, to make green sugar syrup.

Decoration
11. Use the bittersweet chocolate to make fans; see chocolate techniques, p. 34.
12. After coring, finely chop the pineapple with a sharp knife. Cover with plastic wrap and refrigerate.

Serving
13. Arrange the chopped pineapple inside a cookie cutter, directly on the plate, like beef tartar.
14. Using an electric mixer or by hand, whisk the mousse until porous. Dipping a tablespoon in hot water, form an egg-shape of mousse and place on top of the pineapple.
15. Decorate with pineapple and banana slices, and chocolate fans. Pour the green sugar syrup around the pineapple.

Tip
If your kitchen or dining room is cold, you can add some (10%) cooking oil to the chocolate to keep it workable.

Orange Brûlée coated with Valrhona Gran Couva Chocolate Mousse   4 portions

• •

I composed this dessert for a guest appearance at
Erik Lallerstedt's restaurant, Bakficka, in Stockholm.
See photo p. 188.

The 1999 harvest of cocoa beans at San Juan Estate
on Trinidad was quite fantastic. And the chocolate made
from it was extremely popular. Of course, you can use
other kinds of chocolate, but the result will not be quite so
exquisite. You can find Gran Couva chocolate in most
well stocked chocolate or herb stores.

Brûlée

1 sheet gelatin (2 g)
grated zest of 1 orange
7 oz (200 g) freshly squeezed orange juice (about
    4 oranges)
1/2 inch cinnamon stick, from Sri Lanka
2.6 oz (75 g) heavy cream (1/2 cup)
1.4 oz (40 g) crème fraîche, 40% fat
2.8 oz (80 g) egg yolk (about 4 yolks)
1.8 oz (50 g) sugar

Pistachio dacquoise

0.5 oz (15 g) pistachios
0.9 oz (25 g) almonds
1.4 oz (40 g) sugar
1.1 oz (30 g) egg white (about 1 white)
1 drop lemon juice
0.7 oz (20 g) sugar

Gran Couva chocolate mousse

3.7 oz (105 g) bittersweet chocolate (Valrhona Gran Couva
    68% or Marabou dark)
5.3 oz (150 g) heavy cream (3/4 cup)
2.1 oz (60 g) egg yolk (about 3 yolks)
1.6 oz (45 g) sugar
1 tbs water (15 g)

1 orange
2 oz (50 g) sugar

2.6 oz (75 g) white chocolate (Valrhona Ivoire, Callebaut,
    Lindt or Fazer)
0.4 oz (10 g) dark chocolate of your own choice
2 sheets acetate film

Milk chocolate ice cream

See Chocolate Ice Cream, p. 196, but exchange
the bittersweet chocolate for 6 oz milk chocolate
(Valrhona Jivara Lactée 40% or Marabou milk).

DAY 1

Brûlée

1. Soak the gelatin in plenty of cold water for at least 10 minutes.
2. Clean 1 orange and grate off the zest.
3. Squeeze 7 oz orange juice and mix with the zest. Boil until
   3 1/4 oz remains.
4. Add cinnamon, cream and crème fraîche and bring to a boil.
5. Whisk the egg and sugar until light and fluffy.
6. Whisk the orange cream into the egg-sugar mixture.
7. Stirring constantly, heat to 185°F. Do a rose or spoon test;
   see p. 45, if you do not have a thermometer.
8. Drain the gelatin sheet.
9. Put the gelatin in the hot mixture and stir until completely
   dissolved.
10. Sieve the mixture into a bowl. Pour into a flexible plastic ice
    cube tray and freeze.

Pistachio daquoise

11. Preheat oven to 350°F.
12. Using a blender or food processor, pulverize the nuts and
    almonds. Add the sugar, and mix to a fine powder.
13. Whisk the egg white, lemon and sugar until stiff.
14. Sift the nut powder into the mixture.
15. Fold in carefully with a baking spatula.
16. Pipe out 1 1/4 inch circles of meringue mixture on parchment
    paper.
17. Bake for 15–20 minutes. The meringue bases should be brittle
    but still somewhat springy.

Chocolate mousse

18. Chop and melt the chocolate to 131°F, in a microwave oven
    or double boiler.
19. Whip the cream and refrigerate.
20. Whisk together the egg yolk, sugar and water in a bowl.
21. Placing the bowl in a saucepan of boiling water, whisk
    vigorously into a creamy batter, about 185°F.
22. Pass the batter through a fine strainer and continue whisking
    until cool.
23. Mix the hot chocolate and half the whipped cream into a
    ganache. Fold the ganache into the remaining cream and
    mix thoroughly.
24. Fold in the egg batter and whisk to a light, porous mousse.
25. Fill a plastic cone with a no. 10 tip, and pipe out the mousse
    into 4 plastic champagne glasses, until half full. Bang the
    glasses on the table to remove any pockets of air.
26. Loosen the brûlée ice cubes and press a few into each glass.
27. Fill the glasses to the top with mousse, banging on the table.
    Top with a pistachio dacquoise meringue and freeze for at
    least 5 hours, preferably overnight.

Recipe continues on p. 189.

Orange slices in aspic

28. Preheat oven to 400°F.
29. Slice an orange as thinly as possible and place the slices in a container.
30. Cover with hot water and place in the oven for 45 minutes.
31. Pour off the water and cover with 2 oz sugar. Leave to cool.
32. Cover with plastic wrap and refrigerate.

DAY 2 OR LATER SAME DAY

33. Melt both the white and dark chocolate, in a microwave oven or double boiler. Temper the white chocolate; see p. 35. Irregularly stripe the acetate sheet with half the dark chocolate. Spread a thin layer of white chocolate on the sheet and leave until almost hardened. Press out 2 1/2 inch diameter circles. Make a smaller hole in the middle of each circle. Cover with the other sheet of acetate, place a weight on top and refrigerate.
34. To make chocolate bamboo: splash the remaining dark chocolate on a marble slab, or other cold working surface. Spread over with the white chocolate. Roll into bamboo (see chocolate cigarettes, p. 40).
35. Warm the champagne glasses with your hands to release the mousse. Arrange on plates and powder with a little cocoa. Loosen the circles from the film and place on the mousse. Decorate with the chocolate bamboo. Places two slices of orange on each plate. Dipping a tablespoon in hot water, scoop out "eggs" of chocolate mousse and place on the orange slices.

Tip

If you want to give this dessert a velvety look, mix "chocolate spray" using 40% melted chocolate and 60% cocoa butter. Melt the mixture and pass through a strainer. Pour the mixture into a spray gun and decorate the frozen mousse. This is the method the professionals use, but it only works if the dessert is properly frozen. You can also spray molded figures in this way, tempering the chocolate first.

CHAPTER 11

hot
chocolate
desserts

The perfect soufflé should have a melting consistency. It should be creamy inside and have a crispy crust.

Soufflés were the height of fashion in the 1960's and have now made a comeback, both at restaurants and in the home.

Soufflé dishes

I personally prefer individual dishes since they are easier to supervise. Use dishes that are 3 1/2 inch diameter and 2 1/2 inch high. Make soufflés for 4 people at the most, using a 8–9 inch diameter and 2 1/2 inch high dish.

Grease the dishes with a brush. Sprinkle with sugar and twirl the dish to ensure that the sides are fully covered. This will ensure that the soufflé rises correctly and gets a crispy surface. The best way to make sure that the soufflé rises properly and subsequently loosens from the dish, is to freeze the dishes for a few minutes, after greasing and sugaring, and before you pour in the soufflé mixture.

The art of whisking egg whites

The classic way of whisking egg whites is to use an unlined, round copper bowl that has been rubbed with vinegar and salt, before rinsing with cold water. The whisk should be a compact egg white whisk and not a thinner sauce whisk.

Preferably break the eggs the day before serving. The water in the egg white will evaporate, making the meringue stiffer. Cover the egg yolks with plastic wrap so the surface does not dry.

Most people use electric mixers these days, which is excellent. Make sure, however, not to run the mixer at the highest speed initially or the froth will rise too quickly, flocculate and then collapse to a wet soup as soon as you stir the soufflé mixture. This will result in a "cauliflower soufflé" which cracks on the surface. Egg whites should therefore be whisked at medium speed. Egg whites, lemon juice and a 1/3 of the sugar should be whisked by hand with wide arm movements. Tilting the bowl will make it easier to whisk in air.

When the egg white begins to resemble meringue froth, add the remaining sugar. Now it should be whisked at top speed until the meringue froth has stiffened. Do not, however, whisk for too long or the meringue will flocculate—the egg white bubbles have been stretched too much and will collapse when added to the soufflé mixture. The edges will be too hard and the soufflé will not rise as it should.

Always take a quarter of the meringue froth and mix with the batter. Stir to a smooth cream before folding in the remaining meringue froth. Use a pastry spatula when stirring.

Baking soufflés

Divide the soufflé mixture into the dishes and smooth with a spatula. Cut round the edges with a small, sharp knife to ensure that the soufflé will loosen from the edge of the dish.

The soufflés can be prepared 2–4 hours before baking if they are kept in the refrigerator. If you wish to start even earlier, you can freeze the soufflés in the dishes. The unfrozen soufflés should be baked for 15–18 minutes. Always preheat the baking sheet before you place the soufflés in the oven. This will ensure that the heat will immediately come from underneath and that the soufflé will rise evenly.

Chocolate Soufflé—with vanilla ice cream and hot chocolate sauce   about 4 portions

• •

I prefer to use muscovado sugar when making vanilla ice cream. It is a dark, unrefined sugar from Mauritius. Spicy, and with a hint of licorice. It should be available at well-stocked supermarkets and will give your ice cream an exciting flavor.

If you wish to make ordinary vanilla ice cream, just use granulated sugar. I prefer to use vanilla pods from Tahiti; these have so much more flavor than bourbon vanilla.

butter and sugar for lining the dishes

Vanilla ice cream (4–6 portions)
    1 sheet (2 g) gelatin
    1 vanilla pod
    8.8 oz (250 g) heavy cream (1 cup)
    8.8 oz (250 g) milk (1 cup)
    0.9 oz (25 g) honey or glucose
    4.2 oz (120 g) egg yolk (about 6 yolks)
    4.4 oz (125 g) sugar, muscovado sugar or other

Chocolate sauce
    3.5 oz (100 g) bittersweet chocolate (Valrhona Grand Cru
        Guanaja 70.5% or Marabou dark)
    0.7 oz (20 g) unsalted butter
    5.3 oz (150 g) heavy cream (3/4 cup)

Chocolate soufflé
    1.4 oz (40 g) unsalted butter
    1.4 oz (40 g) all purpose flour
    7 oz (200 g) milk (7/8 cup)
    0.9 oz (25 g) high quality cocoa powder, preferably
        Valrhona
    2.8 oz (80 g) egg yolk (about 4 yolks)
    2 tbs dark rum
    5.3 0z (150 g) egg white
    1 tsp freshly squeezed lemon juice
    1.8 oz (50 g) sugar

confectioners' sugar

DAY 1
Make the vanilla ice cream
1. Soak the gelatin in cold water for about 10 minutes.
2. Split the vanilla pod and scrape the seeds into a saucepan. Pour in the cream and milk, add the honey or glucose and vanilla pod.
3. Whisk the egg yolks and sugar until frothy.
4. Boil the cream mixture and pour into the egg froth. Whisk thoroughly and return to the saucepan.
5. Stirring continuously, heat to 185°F. Do a rose or spoon test (see p. 45) if you do not have a thermometer.
6. Drain the gelatin and stir into the hot cream until dissolved.
7. Strain the cream into a bowl. Cool quickly in a saucepan of cold water. Cover with plastic wrap and leave to chill overnight, or preferably 24 hours. (By letting the ice cream mixture mature overnight, you allow the proteins to swell, which will give a creamier and smoother ice cream.)

Recipe continues on next page p. 194.

DAY 2

8. Pour the mixture into the ice cream maker and run for
    30–45 minutes until firm. If you do not have a machine, pour
    the mixture into a bowl and place in the freezer, removing
    occasionally to stir, until firm.

Chocolate sauce

9. Finely chop the chocolate. Cube the butter.
10. Bring the cream to the boil, add the chocolate, stirring
    vigorously. Boil for 30 seconds, continuing to stir vigorously.
11. Whisk in the butter cubes. The sauce should be served at
    85–105°F, and can be kept hot by placing the bowl in a
    saucepan of simmering water.

Chocolate soufflé

12. Butter and sugar 4 individual dishes, 3 1/2 inch diameter and
    2 1/2 inch high.
13. Melt the butter in a saucepan and whisk in the flour. Fry
    briefly.
14. Whisk in the milk and bring to a boil, stirring vigorously.
    Stir thoroughly so that the flour swells.
15. Remove from the heat and sift the cocoa directly into the
    saucepan. Stir thoroughly and leave to cool for 2 minutes.
16. Whisk in the eggs, one at the time. Add the rum.
17. Whisk the egg white, lemon juice and 1/3 of the sugar, using
    an electric mixer at medium speed. You can also whisk by
    hand, using wide arm movements.
18. Add the rest of the sugar and whisk at high speed until stiff.
19. Fold a quarter of the egg white into the egg-cocoa mixture.
    Stir to a smooth cream.
20. Fold in the remaining egg white and mix until smooth, using
    a baking spatula.
21. Divide the mixture evenly among the dishes. If you are making
    only one large soufflé, smooth the top with a spatula.
22. Cut round the edges with a small, sharp knife to ensure the
    soufflé will loosen from the sides of the dishes. Store in the
    refrigerator before baking (2–4 hours at most).

(You can prepare as far as this in advance.)

23. Preheat oven to 350°F.
24. Bake the soufflés. If the soufflé mixture is newly prepared
    and hot, bake for 9 minutes; if it has been refrigerated,
    bake for 12–13 minutes. A large soufflé should be baked for
    20 minutes if the mixture is hot, or 25 minutes if it has been
    refrigerated.
25. Remove from the oven and powder with confectioners' sugar.
26. Let the soufflé rest for 1–2 minutes before turning upside
    down on a plate and removing the dish; see photo on
    opposite page.
27. Serve with hot chocolate sauce and scoops of vanilla ice cream
    in a bowl.

Tip

*If you
wish to use
chocolate in
the soufflé
batter, add
2.8 oz (80 g)
bittersweet
chocolate
instead of
cocoa
powder.*

Mango Soufflé with Valrhona Grand Cru Manjari Ice Cream   6 portions

• •

Try to get hold of really ripe mangoes, preferably from Thailand (these have the strongest aroma).

The first time I baked ice cream in a soufflé was during a guest appearance at Sturehof in Stockholm. This has always been one of Sweden's busiest restaurants, which made it an extra challenge. Sturehof's head chef Kajsa Forsberg had borrowed an extra oven so that we could produce our hot soufflés with their cold surprises in the middle! My helper, the European Sandwich Champion, Linda Nilsson, and I were very tired after this performance.

Chocolate ice cream (4–6 portions)
1 sheet gelatin (2 g)
1 vanilla pod, preferably Tahitian
8.8 oz (250 g) heavy cream (1 cup)
8.8 oz (250 g) milk (1 cup)
4.2 oz (120 g) egg yolk (about 6 yolks)
4.4 oz (125 g) raw sugar or brown sugar
4.4 oz (125 g) bittersweet chocolate (Valrhona Grand Cru Manjari 64.5% or Marabou dark)

Mango soufflé
butter and sugar for lining the dishes
9.5 oz (270 g) mango purée (made from 1 ripe 12 oz mango, or 2 smaller ones)
1.1 oz (30 g) sugar
2 tbs freshly squeezed lemon juice
0.4 oz (12 g) potato flour
4 tbs (20 g) white rum
5.3 oz (150 g) egg white (about 5 whites)
1 tbs freshly squeezed lemon juice
1.8 oz (50 g) sugar

confectioners' sugar

DAY 1
Chocolate ice cream
1. Soak the gelatin in cold water for about 10 minutes.
2. Split the vanilla pod and scrape the seeds into a saucepan. Pour in the cream and milk, add the honey or glucose and vanilla pod.
3. Whisk the egg yolks and sugar until frothy.
4. Boil up the cream mixture, remove the vanilla pod, and whisk into the egg froth. Blend thoroughly and return to the saucepan.

5. Finely chop the chocolate and add.
6. Stirring continuously, heat the chocolate cream to 185°F. Do a rose or spoon test (see p. 45) if you do not have a thermometer.
7. Drain the gelatin and stir into the hot cream until dissolved.
8. Pour the cream through a fine strainer into a bowl. Cover with plastic wrap and refrigerate overnight.

DAY 2
9. Pour the mixture into an ice cream maker and run for 30–45 minutes until firm. If you do not have a machine, pour the mixture into a bowl and place in the freezer, removing occasionally to stir, until firm.

Mango soufflé
10. Butter and sugar 6 soufflé dishes, 3 1/2 inch diameter and 2 1/2 inch high. Place in the freezer.
11. Peel the mango and cut out 9 1/2 oz ripe flesh.
12. Mix the mango, sugar and lemon juice to a purée, in a blender. Pass the purée through a fine strainer.
13. Mix the mango purée and potato flour in a saucepan. Heat up, stirring continuously, and boil to a jam consistency.
14. Add the rum, stirring with a baking spatula. Cover with plastic wrap.
15. Using an electric mixer at medium speed, whisk the egg white, lemon juice and 1/3 of the sugar to a soft froth. Add the remaining sugar and mix, at maximum speed, until stiff.
16. Fold 1/4 of the egg white into the mango jam. Stir to a smooth paste.
17. Fold in the remaining egg white, using a baking spatula, and stir until light.
18. Half fill the frozen soufflé dishes with the mixture.
19. Dip a large tablespoon in hot water and scoop out "eggs" of chocolate ice cream and place in the middle of each dish. Return the dishes to the freezer.
20. Remove one dish at a time and fill them with soufflé mixture. It is important that the mixture runs around the ice cream to insulate it when baking. Smooth off the top of the dishes with a spatula. Using a small knife, loosen the soufflé mixture from the edge of the dishes.
21. Freeze the dishes for at least 6 hours before baking, or else the ice cream will melt.

At least 6 hours later

22. Preheat oven to 350°F.
23. Transfer the soufflé dishes directly from the freezer to a preheated baking sheet in the oven. Bake for 15–20 minutes until the soufflé has risen.
24. Powder with confectioners' sugar and serve immediately.

Tip

*Raspberry sorbet also makes
a good filling for this soufflé.*

Hot Chocolate Cake—with liquid pistachio ganache and chocolate sorbet

4 portions

• •

The tangy Manjari chocolate makes the perfect foil for the pistachio flavor. See photo, p. 198.

Four cake rings, about 3 1/4 inch diameter and 1 1/4 inch high, for the pistachio ganache. Butter for greasing.

Chocolate sorbet
- 1 sheet gelatin (2 g)
- 2.6 0z (75 g) sugar
- 1 cup mineral water
- 1.8 oz (50 g) honey
- 1.8 oz (50 g) bittersweet chocolate (Valrhona Grand Cru Guanaja 70.5% or Marabou dark)
- 1.8 oz (50 g) cocoa powder
- 5.3 oz (150 g) milk (3/4 cup)

Pistachio ganache
- 1.8 oz (50 g) white chocolate (Valrhona Ivoire, Callebaut, Lindt or Fazer)
- 1.8 oz (50 g) heavy cream (1/4 cup)
- 0.9 oz (25 g) orange-flower honey
- 1 drop dark rum
- 2 drops orange-flower oil

confectioners' sugar

Chocolate bisquit
- 4.4 oz (125 g) bittersweet chocolate (Valrhona Grand Cru Manjari 64.5% or Marabou dark)
- 0.7 oz (20 g) unsalted butter
- 0.7 oz (20 g) egg yolk (about 1 yolk)
- 0.5 oz (15 g) cornstarch (about 1 tsp)
- 3.2 oz (90 g) egg white (about 3 whites)
- 1 tsp lemon juice
- 0.9 oz (25 g) sugar

DAY 1

Preparation of chocolate sorbet; see white chocolate sorbet in the recipe for Chocolate Beignet Soufflé, p. 201.

Pistachio ganache
1. Grease the cake rings with butter and place them in the freezer on a baking sheet.
2. Finely chop the chocolate. Boil together the cream and honey and pour it over the chocolate. Stir with a baking spatula to a smooth ganache.
3. Pulverize the pistachios in a blender or food processor. Fold the pistachio powder into the ganache and add rum and orange-flower oil. Pour into a small, low metal container and freeze for at least 4 hours.

Chocolate bisquit
4. Finely chop the bittersweet chocolate. Melt in a microwave oven or double boiler, while stirring. Heat to 131°F.
5. Stir in the butter until melted, then add the egg yolk.
6. Sift the cornstarch onto a paper.
7. Whisk the egg white, lemon and sugar until firm, using an electric mixer at medium speed.
8. Fold the egg white mixture into the melted chocolate, using a baking spatula. Finally, fold in the cornstarch.
9. Half fill the cake rings with chocolate batter.

10. Remove the frozen ganache and divide into 4 equal pieces. Place one piece in the middle of each ring.
11. Top up with the remaining batter.
12. Freeze for at least 4 hours before serving.

DAY 2 OR LATER SAME DAY
13. Preheat oven to 350°F.
14. Transfer the cake rings directly from the freezer to a preheated baking sheet in the oven. Bake for 12–15 minutes, until they have risen properly.
15. Transfer the cakes onto 4 hot plates and leave for 5 minutes to stabilize.
16. Carefully lift the cakes and make a deep cut with a knife. Powder with confectioners' sugar and serve immediately.
17. Try to freeze the sorbet as late as possible and serve with the cakes.

Elderberry Flower Beignet   4 portions

• •

A delicious, crispy summer dessert served with caramelized milk chocolate mousse and elderberry sabayon. Preferably use green cardamom, which is a bit more rounded and sharp in taste. Available from herb stores.

12 large elderberry flowers
caramelized milk chocolate with cardamom
7 oz (200 g) heavy cream (7/8 cup)
1.1 oz (30 g) sugar
2.1 oz (60 g) milk chocolate (Valrhona Jivara Lactée 40%
    or Marabou milk)
1 tsp ground cardamom

Chocolate Beignet dough
3.5 oz (100 g) all-purpose flour
1 tsp (5 g) vanilla sugar
25 g cocoa powder
1 tbs peanut oil
1/2 tsp salt
2/3 cup porter beer
2 tbs milk
0.7 oz (20 g) egg yolk (about 1 yolk)
a few drops of vinegar
pinch of salt
1.1 oz (30 g) egg white (about 1 white)
1 tsp (5 g) sugar

Elderberry Sabayon
2/3 cup elderberry juice
1/4 cup freshly squeezed lemon juice
2.1 oz (60 g) sugar
2.8 oz (80 g) egg yolk (about 4 yolks)

2 cups cooking oil

Caramelized milk chocolate mousse with cardamom
1. Boil up half the cream for the mousse.
2. Melt the sugar until golden and slightly smoking. Pour in the hot cream and stir until the caramel has completely dissolved.
3. Finely chop the chocolate and stir into the mixture until melted.
4. Add the remaining cold cream with the cardamom. Using a hand blender, mix until smooth.
5. Strain the mixture into a bowl and cover with plastic wrap. Leave in the refrigerator to "swell" for at least 3 hours.

Chocolate beignet dough
6. Sift the flour, confectioners' sugar and cocoa into a bowl. Add oil, salt, porter, milk and egg yolk. Mix until smooth.
7. Cover with plastic wrap and leave for 2 hours in the refrigerator to swell.
8. Using a little vinegar and salt, rub a metal or copper bowl absolutely clean. Whisk the egg white and sugar in the bowl until stiff.
9. Using a baking spatula, fold the egg white into the refrigerated mixture.

Sabayon sauce
10. Fill a saucepan 1/3 full with water and bring to a boil.
11. Whisk together all the ingredients in a metal bowl. Place the bowl in the boiling water.
12. Whisk constantly until the sauce begins to thicken.
13. Serve the sauce hot from a warm sauceboat.
14. Remove the mousse from the refrigerator. Using an electric mixer, whisk the cold mousse to the same consistency as whipped cream. Do not whisk too long or the mousse will curdle.
15. Dip a large spoon in warm water. Scoop out a large "egg" of mousse and place on one side of the plate. Garnish with a sprig of elderberry.
16. Heat the oil to 350°F in a frying pan, or deep fryer.
17. Dip the flowers in the chocolate beignet batter. Fry a few at a time until brown and crispy. Leave to drain on kitchen paper. Arrange on the plates and serve with the hot sauce.

Chocolate Beignet Soufflé   4 portions

•

Beignet soufflé is a delicious, but somewhat forgotten, dessert. We often used to make different versions of this soufflé at the Savoy Hotel in Malmö. We usually filled them with apple compote, rolled them in cinnamon sugar and served with cold vanilla custard. See photo, p. 202.

1 batch vanilla cream, crème patisserie; see Othello p. 132

1 batch chocolate pâte à choux; see Chocolate Éclairs, p. 136

White chocolate sorbet
    1 sheet gelatin (2 g)
    2.6 oz (75 g) sugar
    8.8 oz (250 g) mineral water (1 cup)
    1.8 oz (50 g) apple-flower honey
    5.3 oz (150 g) white chocolate (Valrhona Ivoire, Lindt,
        Fazer or Callebaut)
    8.8 oz (250 g) milk, 3% fat (1 cup)
    8.8 oz (250 g) Cointreau (1 cup) liqueur
    2 cups cooking oil

1. Make vanilla cream and leave to cool.
2. Make the pâte à choux mixture. Using a plastic pastry bag with a smooth no. 8 tip, pipe out 16 balls onto parchment paper and leave to stiffen in the refrigerator.

White chocolate sorbet
3. Soak the gelatin for 10 minutes in cold water.
4. Boil together the sugar, mineral water and honey into sugar syrup.
5. Remove the gelatin from the water and, without draining, stir into the sugar syrup until dissolved.
6. Chop the chocolate and stir into the sugar syrup until melted.
7. Pass through a fine strainer. Add the milk and Cointreau and whisk thoroughly.
8. Run the mixture for 30–45 minutes in an ice cream maker, until firm. Or you can place the mixture in the freezer and stir occasionally.
9. Heat the oil to 350°F, in a frying pan or deep fryer. Remove the balls from the parchment paper and fry them in 3 batches, until they have swollen and are light brown. This should take about 2 minutes. Remove and leave to drain on double kitchen paper.
10. Make a hole in each ball and fill them with vanilla cream, with the help of a spoon. Arrange 4 balls on each plate and serve with sorbet.

Hot Chocolate Mousse with Coffee Ice Cream   4 portions

•

Valrhona's Chuao chocolate from Venezuela (vintage 1999), with its unique beans from the Chuao valley, gave me a fantastic desire to create new desserts. This hot and cold mousse, with creamy coffee ice cream, reminds me of South America. See photo, p. 203.

4 ovenproof coffee cups

    butter and sugar for lining the cups
    confectioners' sugar

Coffee ice cream
    1 sheet gelatin (2 g)
    8.8 oz (250 g) milk
    8.8 oz (250 g) heavy cream (1 cup)
    0.9 oz (25 g) honey, preferably acacia
    0.9 oz (25 g) ground espresso beans
    3.5 oz (100 g) milk chocolate (Valrhona Jivara Lactée 40%
        or Marabou milk)
    4.2 oz (120 g) egg yolk (about 6 yolks)
    3.5 oz (100 g) raw sugar

Caramelized walnuts
    2.6 oz (75 g) walnuts
    0.5 oz (15 g) confectioners' sugar
    1 drop lemon juice
    1 tsp butter

Banana slivers
    1/2 batch basic sugar syrup; see Pineapple Tartar, p. 185
    4 lengthwise slices of unripe banana

Valrhona Chuao chocolate mousse
    3.5 oz (100 g) bittersweet chocolate (Valrhona Chuao 65%
        or Marabou dark)
    0.9 oz (25 g) unsalted butter, room temperature
    2.1 oz (60 g) egg yolk (about 3 yolks)
    1 tbs Cointreau or Grand Marnier liqueur
    3.2 oz (90 g) egg white (about 3 whites)
    1 tsp freshly squeezed lemon juice
    1.8 oz (50 g) sugar

Recipe continues on p. 204.

DAY 1

Coffee ice cream

1. Soak the gelatin for 10 minutes in cold water.
2. Mix the milk, cream, honey and coffee beans in a saucepan and bring to a boil. Remove from the heat and leave to set for 5 minutes. Pour through a fine strainer into a saucepan.
3. Finely chop the chocolate and add to the mixture. Whisk the egg yolk and sugar until light and frothy.
4. Add the egg froth to the mixture and heat, stirring constantly, to 185°F. If you do not have a thermometer, do a rose or spoon test; see p. 45.
5. Drain the gelatin sheet, add to the mixture and stir until dissolved. Pass the mixture through a fine strainer into a bowl. Cool quickly by placing the bowl in a saucepan of cold water. Cover with plastic wrap.
6. Refrigerate for 24 hours.

DAY 2

Caramelized walnuts

7. Put the walnuts, confectioners' sugar and lemon juice in a saucepan and heat. Stir until the caramel is golden. Add the butter and pour out onto a sheet of parchment paper and leave to cool. Crush coarsely with a rolling pin.
8. Run the ice cream mixture for 30–45 minutes in an ice cream maker until firm. If you do not have a machine, place the mixture in the freezer and stir occasionally. Fold the crushed walnuts into the ice cream.
9. Make 1/2 batch of basic sugar syrup; see Pineapple Tartar, p. 185, and coat the banana slices.

Chocolate mousse

10. Grease 4 coffee cups with butter and sprinkle with sugar.
11. Finely chop the chocolate and heat to 131°F, in a microwave oven or double boiler. Stir in the butter until melted and then add the egg yolks and liqueur.
12. Stir with a baking spatula to a smooth, pliable ganache.
13. Whisk the egg white, lemon juice and 1/3 sugar to a soft froth, using an electric mixer at medium speed or by hand with wide arm movements.
14. Add the remaining sugar and whisk at maximum speed until stiff.
15. Mix 1/4 of the egg white with chocolate ganache and then fold the mixture into the remaining egg white. Use a baking spatula, and mix until light and porous.
16. Divide the mousse evenly into the coffee cups. Smooth off with a spatula, and freeze for at least 4 hours.

FOUR HOURS LATER

17. Preheat oven to 350°F.
18. Bake for 8 minutes. Powder with confectioners' sugar and serve immediately with coffee ice cream decorated with banana slices, and maybe a dollop of whipped cream.

Hot Chocolate Soup with Pineapple Skewers   4 portions

●

1 large fresh pineapple, Del Monte extra sweet

0.9 oz (25 g) unsalted butter for frying the pineapple

Chocolate soup

12.3 oz (350 g) milk (1 1/2 cups)
5.3 oz (150 g) whipped cream (3/4 cup)
1 vanilla pod
1 tsp sea salt, fleur de sel
1/2 inch cinnamon from Sri Lanka
4 anise stars
1 orange
1 jalapeño chili
5.3 oz (150 g) bittersweet chocolate (Valrhona Chuao 65% or Marabou dark)
2 tsp dark rum

1. Peel the pineapple carefully and remove any brown spots. Divide into 4 and remove the core.
2. Cut 4 large pieces for each person. Soak 4 wooden skewers in water.
3. Spear the pineapple chunks onto the skewers.

Chocolate soup

4. Pour milk and cream into a saucepan. Split the vanilla pod and scrape out the seeds.
5. Put the seeds, salt, cinnamon and anise stars in the saucepan and bring to a boil.
6. Wash the orange and zest half. Divide the chili lengthwise and remove the seeds. Use plastic gloves to avoid getting burned! Add the chili and orange zest to the soup and cover with a lid. Leave to draw for 30 minutes.
7. Pour the soup through a fine strainer and bring back to the boil. Add the chopped chocolate. Using a hand blender or food processor, mix the soup until frothy. Add the rum.
8. Brown the butter and fry the pineapple until golden brown.
9. Pour the frothy soup into individual bowls and serve with the pineapple skewers on top.

drinking chocolate

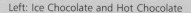
Left: Ice Chocolate and Hot Chocolate

Hot Chocolate 6 cups

1 cup whipped cream for topping

1 vanilla pod
3 cups milk
1 1/4 cup heavy cream
3 1/2 oz bittersweet chocolate (Valrhona Grand Cru
    Guanaja 70.5% or Marabou dark)

1. Split the vanilla pod and scrape the seeds into a saucepan.
    Add the cream, milk and vanilla pod.
2. Bring to the boil and strain into another saucepan. Add the
    chopped chocolate and stir with a whisk until melted.
3. Whip the cream.
4. Froth the chocolate with a hand blender. Pour into cups and
    pipe the whipped cream on top. Powder with cocoa.

Hot Spicy Chocolate

Same recipe as above, but adding:
    1 finely chopped chili, with the seeds removed
    4 anise stars
    1 inch cinnamon from Sri Lanka
    1 tsp saffron
    1 tbs sea salt, fleur de sel
    1 oz apple-flower honey

Add the spices to the milk and cream at the same time as the
vanilla pod. Put a lid on the saucepan and leave to set before
straining.

Quick Hot Chocolate 6 cups

4 1/2 cups milk
1 3/4 oz cocoa powder, preferably Valrhona
1 3/4 oz sugar

1. Boil the milk in a saucepan.
2. Mix the cocoa and sugar and add to the milk. Mix until frothy,
    using a hand blender.
3. Pour out and serve.

If you have a cappuccino frother you can top the chocolate with
frothed milk.

Hot Chocolate with Rum

Pour 1/4 cup dark rum in each cup of chocolate. Top with whipped
cream and powder with cocoa.

50/50

Half hot chocolate and half espresso.

Russian Chocolate

Pour 1/2 cup cognac in each tumbler and fill with hot chocolate.
Top with whipped cream and powder with cocoa.

Irish Chocolate

Pour 1/2 cup Irish whiskey in each tumbler. Add 1 tbs honey and
fill with hot chocolate. Top with whipped cream and powder with
cocoa.

Ice Chocolate

See photo below

Place 2 large scoops of vanilla ice cream in a tall glass. Fill with chilled hot chocolate, see first recipe. Decorate with whipped cream and powder with cocoa.

Martinique Ice Chocolate

Place 2 large scoops of banana ice cream in each tumbler. Add 1/4 cup dark rum and fill the glass with chilled hot chocolate (see recipe 1). Decorate with whipped cream and powder with cocoa.

Havanna Ice Chocolate

Place 2 large scoops of coffee ice cream in each tumbler. Add 1/4 cup dark rum and fill the glass with chilled hot chocolate (see recipe 1). Decorate with whipped cream and powder with cocoa.

Singapore Ice Chocolate

Place 2 large scoops of coconut ice cream in each tumbler. Top up with equal amounts of pineapple juice and chilled hot chocolate (see recipe 1). Decorate with whipped cream and powder with cocoa.

Kir au Chocolat

1/4 cup Crème de Cassis, French black currant liqueur
2/3 cup red Burgundy
1 scoop chocolate sorbet

Mix the chilled wine with the liqueur. Place a scoop of chocolate sorbet in the glass.

Lumumba

Pour 1/2 cup cognac in a tumbler. Fill with ice and chilled hot chocolate (see recipe 1).

CHAPTER 13

chocolate
menus

Making food spiced with chocolate can give rise to new, exciting combinations and taste experiences. Cocoa of the highest quality (which does not taste sweet) is often used, as are peeled and roasted cocoa beans, which will give both flavor and crispness. Bittersweet chocolate with 70% cocoa can also be used and will not sweeten the food too much.

White chocolate can also work, but it must be balanced with acidity, as in the following soup recipe. Chili also combines well with chocolate.

Together with some gourmet friends, I devised and prepared this chocolate menu for 6 people.

Dare to use chocolate in food—it'll give you some exciting new taste experiences!

Grilled Duck Liver—with cocoa beans, pineapple, grapes, and hot chocolate brioche

Grill the duck liver quickly so that the liver does not lose too much fat.

21 oz fresh duck liver (you can use frozen)
1 fresh pineapple, Del Monte extra sweet
7 oz green grapes
3.5 oz cocoa beans
2 tbs sugar cane
1 tbs dark rum
gourmet salt
freshly ground white pepper

6 brioches; see Chocolate Brioche p. 108

1. Peel 7 oz pineapple and cut into small cubes. Rinse and divide the grapes. Remove the pips and peel, using a teaspoon.
2. Roast the cocoa beans in a frying pan until the peel begins to loosen. Remove the peels and crush the beans in a mortar.
3. Cut the fresh duck liver into 12 slices. Remove any membrane or blood vessels, using a knife.
4. Quickly grill the duck liver in the hot frying pan. Duck liver should be browned somewhat. Spice with salt and pepper and leave to drain on kitchen paper.
5. Melt the sugar to caramel in the frying pan. Add the cocoa beans and pineapple and sauté until slightly browned.
6. Flambé with rum (mind your hands!). Add the grapes and heat.
7. Serve the duck liver on hot plates. Sprinkle with salt and pepper, pour over the caramelized fruit and serve immediately with hot chocolate brioches.

Mussel Soup—spiced with saffron and white chocolate

1 lb fresh blue mussels
12 live river crayfish or fresh unshelled sea crayfish
3/4 cup (120 g) finely chopped shallots
3 large crushed cloves garlic
2 tbs (30 g) unsalted butter
1 tbs olive oil
1 tbs tomato purée
4 1/2 cups chicken stock
2 cups dry white wine
freshly ground white pepper

Soup

9 oz fennel
3 1/2 oz leek
3 1/2 oz carrot
3 tbs (30 g) unsalted butter
1 vanilla pod
1/2 tsp saffron
3 oz white chocolate, preferably Valrhona Ivoire (which isn't too sweet)
1 1/4 cup heavy cream
salt and ground white pepper

Marinated mussels

half the mussels
grated zest of 1 lemon
1 crushed clove garlic
parsley
2 tbs virgin olive oil

1. Mussel stock: scrape the mussels well and brush thoroughly under cold, running water. Cut off the "beard" with a sharp knife.
2. Throw away any mussels that do not close when you knock them.
3. In a 5-quart saucepan on low heat, sauté the finely chopped shallots and garlic in the butter and oil. Make sure they do not get brown. Roast the tomato purée for about 1 minute.
4. Tip the mussels and the crayfish into the saucepan. Grind some white pepper directly into the pan. Pour in the boiling chicken stock and wine. Increase the heat and put on the lid.

5. Quickly boil up the mussels. Let them boil until they open (about 5 minutes) and this will give you perfect stock.
6. Using a perforated ladle, remove the mussels and crayfish and put them in the refrigerator.
7. Strain the stock.
8. Sauté the chopped fennel, leak and carrot in butter for a few minutes. Add the stock and simmer for about 30 minutes.
9. Split the vanilla pod and scrape the seeds into the soup with the saffron and chopped chocolate.
10. Shell the mussels and place half of them in the soup.
11. Run the soup in a blender or food processor, adding cream, and flavoring with salt and pepper. Pass through a fine strainer.
12. Mix the remaining mussels with the grated lemon zest, crushed garlic, 2 tbs finely chopped parsley, salt, pepper and a few drops of virgin olive oil. Serve spoonfuls of mussels with the soup and a small hot chocolate brioche, if you so wish.
13. Re-boil the soup and pour it into hot bowls. Sprinkle with parsley and serve with the mussels.

Mussels ready for preparation.

Eel Fricassé—with coconut milk, cocoa, chili, and lima beans

This dish is somewhat reminiscent of the classic French eel matelotte.

2 lbs fresh eels
2 tbs all-purpose flour
3 tbs peanut oil
3/4 cup (120 g) finely chopped shallots
6 crushed cloves garlic
2 finely chopped green chilies
2 cups coconut milk
2 cups dry white wine
4 tbs cocoa powder, preferably Valrhona
1 1/2 oz bittersweet chocolate (Valrhona Grand Cru
    Manjari 64%)
salt and freshly ground white pepper
a few drops green Tabasco
4 tbs finely chopped fresh coriander
2 salted lemon peels (to be found in Arabian stores)

1. Divide the skinned and gutted eels into 6 equal pieces. Season with salt and pepper and roll in flour.
2. Heat up the oil in a pot and fry the eel until light brown. Add the shallot and garlic and lower the heat. Sauté for about 5 minutes until the shallot is transparent but not brown.

3. Add chili, coconut milk, white wine, cocoa and chocolate. Put on the lid and braise for about 20 minutes.
4. Remove the pieces of eel and keep them hot.
5. Season the sauce with salt, pepper and green Tabasco.
6. Strain the sauce, put in the pieces of eel and heat gently.
7. Serve in hot, deep plates. Sprinkle with finely chopped coriander, a little salt and lemon. Serve with lima beans.

Boiled lima beans

1 lb lima beans
2 cups water
2 tbs unsalted butter
salt and freshly ground white pepper

1. Pod the beans and remove the outer peel with a knife. Boil the water with 1 tsp salt, put in the beans and boil for 5 minutes.
2. Pour into a colander and drain. Return the beans to the saucepan and add butter, salt and pepper.

Chocolate Sorbet with Armagnac

Sorbet, see p. 199
Serve the sorbet in small, chilled glasses as a middle course. Spoon over 1 tbs Armagnac before serving.

The eel is skinned, cleaned and ready for preparation.

Removing the outer skin from the lima beans.

Wild Duck—twice over

Wild duck is one of my favorite birds. The intense, gamey flavor combines excellently with chocolate, black currants and raspberries. Braise the legs and serve them later as a salad, since they take much longer to prepare than the breasts. The potatoes should be buttery and melting.

3 plucked and drawn wild ducks (about 1 lb 12 oz each)
butter and oil for frying
salt and freshly ground white pepper

Braised legs

legs of the ducks
2 tbs unsalted butter
2 tbs olive oil
3 1/2 oz carrots
3 1/2 oz shallots
3 1/2 oz root celery
3 crushed cloves garlic
1 1/4 cups robust red wine
salt and freshly ground white pepper
thyme
2 tbs cocoa powder, preferably Valrhona
1 tbs unsalted butter
2 tbs olive oil

Chocolate sauce with black currant and raspberries

bodies of the ducks
7 oz raspberries
3 1/2 oz black currants
2 cups dark stock
3/4 cup dry white wine
3/4 cup heavy cream
3 oz bittersweet chocolate (Valrhona Grand Cru Manjari 64%)
2 tbs unsalted butter

Pommes fondante

6 large, equally sized spool-shaped potatoes
7 oz butter
salt and freshly ground white pepper

Sautéd chanterelles

1 1/2 lb fresh chanterelles
4 tbs butter (about 60 g)
salt and freshly ground white pepper

Boiled snow peas

7 oz snow peas, with strings removed
2 cups water
1 tbs unsalted butter
salt and pepper

4 oz raspberries and 4 oz black currants for garnishing

Chanterelles, cleaned and ready for preparation.

Wild duck with chocolate sauce, pommes fondantes, sautéd chanterelles and snow peas—ready to enjoy.

Vinaigrette

3 tbs balsamic vinegar
2 tbs liquid honey
1 tsp dark Dijon mustard
9 tbs virgin olive oil
salt and pepper
2 tbs pine nuts

Lettuce, two kinds that you like best. I chose maché and radicchio.

STEP 1

1. Preheat oven to 475°F. Melt the butter and pour oil into a roasting pan. Place in the oven.
2. Rub the ducks with salt and pepper, inside and out. Cut away the legs. When the butter has stopped bubbling, coat the ducks in the fat. Sauté for about 10 minutes on each side and then for 10–15 minutes skin side down. The total cooking time should be about 30–35 minutes. Baste occasionally.
3. Remove the ducks, and pour the meat juice into the roasting pan.
4. Leave to stand for 15 minutes. Cut away the breasts and wrap in aluminum foil. Place in the refrigerator.

5. **Braise the legs:** Clean and finely chop the vegetables. In a second roasting pan, sauté the vegetables in 2 tbs butter and 2 tbs oil. Add the duck legs and wine. Flavor with salt, freshly ground white pepper, a sprig of thyme and cocoa.
6. Lower the oven to 250°F. Cover the roasting pan and braise in the oven for at least 2 hours.

7. **Make the sauce:** Divide the remains of the bodies into smaller pieces and gently sauté in the first roasting pan for a few minutes. Pour in the stock, wine and berries and simmer for 30 minutes. Strain the sauce and press out the liquid with the backside of a spoon.
8. Add the cream and flavor the sauce with the finely chopped chocolate, salt and pepper. Round off with 2 tbs unsalted butter. Froth up the sauce before serving.

9. **Pommes fondante:** Gently sauté the potatoes in butter, and season with salt and freshly ground white pepper. Braise in butter, under a lid, until they have softened. Pour off the excess butter.
10. Clean the chanterelles and sauté them in butter until golden brown. Season with salt and freshly ground white pepper.

11. Boil up the water with 1 tsp salt. Boil the snow peas for 1 minute.
12. Drain in a colander. Return to the saucepan and sprinkle with a little white pepper and salt and glaze with butter.

13. Heat the breasts in foil, at 250°F for about 20 minutes or until they are heated through.
14. Carve the breasts and place them on hot plates. Garnish with raspberries and black currants. Arrange the potatoes, chanterelles and snow peas around the meat. Serve with a little sauce.

STEP 2

1. Rinse the lettuce and shake off excess water.
2. Whisk together the ingredients for vinaigrette. Drizzle the lettuce with vinaigrette and arrange on plates.
3. Brown the braised duck legs in oil until they have a crisp surface. Place a leg on each plate.
4. Brown 2 tbs pine nuts and sprinkle over the legs, which should have a consistency reminiscent of oxtail.

Dessert

Chocolate terrine with peppermint Anglaise; see recipe p. 182.

Braised duck leg on a bed of lettuce.

CHAPTER 14

What to drink with chocolate

To Jan Hedh
By Michel Jamais

I must be the happiest man in the world, particularly when I can combine my two serious passions in life—wine and chocolate! Old wine snobs may turn in their graves or look down their noses, because chocolate was long perceived as the enemy. Luckily, these old fogies will soon have disappeared and this misconception can be righted—chocolate and wine is a combination made in heaven!

Previously, desserts were a matter of course at any meal, and should be so even today, despite modern healthy living and calorie phobia. But unfortunately too many people forgo a dessert, even though the taste for sweetness is making a comeback. Those who may have fallen for the divine temptation of ice cream, cakes, puddings or chocolate have desisted from complementing them with a sweet wine. "It's just too much sweetness!" one guest might protest. Another will want to continue with the red wine they were drinking previously. Whether or not this stems from pure stinginess, the result can often be murder! The fruitiness and discrete sweetness of a dry white wine or red wine is effectively reduced by the sweetness in the dessert, leaving only roughness and sharp acidity in its place. Ugh!

A simple explanation of this lack of interest in dessert wines—even though many people like them—is a lack of knowledge, not only of these wines in themselves but also how they can be combined with desserts. My ambition here is to change all this! Let us begin with some fundamental advice on the choice of dessert wines.

The one, overriding rule is that the dessert wine should always be sweeter than the dessert itself. Otherwise the wine will seem dry and sour, not particularly pleasant at all. You should therefore taste and judge the relative sweetness of the wine. Here are a few examples:

- An ordinary table wine has about 0.1–0.2 oz residual sugar
- A Sauternes, about 3–3 1/2 oz residual sugar
- A ruby port wine, about 3–4 oz residual sugar
- A German or Austrian trockenbeerenauslese, about 5–9 oz residual sugar
- A Pedro Ximenéz sherry, about 7–14 oz residual sugar

How to solve this problem? You either choose a wine with a pronounced astringency (as in some fortified wines such as port) or else you add an ingredient to the dessert which catches and mellows the astringency. These include ice cream, cream and other high-fat consistencies, or sweet/sour sauces such as cherry.

The balance between the dessert and the wine is important and you must choose a wine with the correct body. The flavors of both the wine and the dessert should be discernable when the two meet. A sorbet is often light, whereas a chocolate dessert can be much heavier. This makes many fortified wines unassailable as a compliment to chocolate. There are, however, many more kinds than just port wines or Madeira. The sweeter the wine, the more body it appears to have.

Finally there are the aromas, all the scent components from both the chocolate and the other ingredients in the dessert. I always aim for total harmony by letting the aromas of the wine reflect the aromas in the dessert. Here are a few examples of how some of the most common ingredients in a dessert can influence your choice of wine:

- Tropical yellow fruit—choose intense wines made from botrytis-infected grapes, such as Sauternes or trockenbeerenauslese.
- Cherry or other red fruit—choose red, fortified wines or recioto from Italy
- Prunes or raisins—choose dark, sweet, full-bodied, well-matured fortified wines
- Chocolate—choose smooth, full-bodied, dark fortified wines
- Nuts—choose sweet, oxidized fortified wines

Always make a general assessment of the dessert—sweetness, intensity, bitterness, creaminess (if there is any), fruit and nut aromas—this will soon make you a master at creating exciting wine and chocolate compositions!

Sweet chocolate wines

When you have orientated yourself in the basic rules of dessert wines, you will soon find that it is not particularly difficult to match wine and chocolate. Just remember that the more cocoa bitterness your dessert has, the more careful you need to be. Sugar, cream and butter, fruit and berries change the characteristics of the chocolate and make it easier to match.

Most people would spontaneously recommend a port wine to chocolate, but beware "vintage" and "late bottled vintage" ports; these often are experienced as too tart when they encounter cocoa. These kinds of port are usually only really good at ten to fifteen years. One way to mitigate the astringency of a wine is to combine it with a sweet/sour red fruit. This mellows the wine, making it seem sweeter and smoother, while reflecting the fruitiness of the wine. A barrel-matured tawny port is a safer alternative. These wines have been refined by maturing in oak barrels, become more rounded, and a complex nutty taste has nestled among the aromas of toffee, caramel and red fruit.

Madeira is also well suited to wine since these wines are never tannic. The delicious undertone of caramel, which originates from the warm storage temperature, make it an excellent accompaniment to any kind of chocolate containing nuts or nougat. You should choose the absolute sweetest kinds of Madeira wine—boal or malmsey. The latter is exquisite in combination with intense chocolate desserts or bittersweet chocolate on its own. A sherry can be just as exciting to serve, whether it is a sweet, nutty oloroso (cream sherry) or a more full-bodied PX sherry from the Pedro Ximenéz grape. The latter must be considered one of the best wines for complementing really heavy chocolate desserts. The explanation is simple—the grapes have firstly been sun dried for up to two weeks and lost half their moisture. The remaining grape is extremely concentrated and sweet, just like the resulting wine. Sometimes the wines are so concentrated they can be served as a sauce, with chocolate ice cream or a brownie!

Besides these three main kinds of fortified wine, there are excellent varieties from all over the world. South African or Australian interpretations of their Portuguese prototypes

are sometimes even better, since they don't have the same astringent backbone and often have a juicier grape.

We can find many brilliant chocolate wines in Australia. The Rutherglen district in northeast Victoria is renown for its dark, intense fortified wines made from Muscat grapes, such as Liqueur Tokay or Liqueur Muscat. The grapes are very ripe and sweet when harvested, which gives a fantastic concentration to the taste, which is further strengthened by years of maturing in oak barrels.

Muscadel Red from South Africa is another trump card. There are several varieties of this wine. Some are made from completely un-fermented grape juice, fortified with liquor and stored, which produces intensely fruity wines. Others are made like traditional port wines (partly fermented, then fortified with brandy). The Muscadel wines I tend to choose have been rounded off in large oak barrels for anything up to a decade. This gives them an almost sinful chocolaty aroma—still seductively Muscat, but more complex. It's just made for all kinds of chocolate desserts. Aaaah! And if that's not enough, they are almost ridiculously cheap in comparison to other wines of similar quality.

But there are, in fact, even cheaper chocolate favorites, such as Commandaria from Cyprus. This I consider to be one of the undiscovered treasures in the world of wine. It is made from grapes that have dried in the sun for up to two weeks, which gives the wine a superb body, and then produced like port wine. After maturing a few years in oak barrels, the wine has developed a wonderfully complex aroma, with dark syrup, nuts, chocolate and blood oranges as the chief components. It has a pronounced sweetness and stands its ground with most chocolate desserts. That they only cost half as much as other port wines should be enough to convince most consumers! If there's any left in the bottle, it can keep for almost a year.

Mavrodaphne of Patras, from Greece, is somewhat simpler but compares favorably with other famous chocolate wines such as Banyul and Maury. The latter originate in Rousillon, just north of the Spanish border, on the Riviera's west flank. They are both examples of vins doux naturels, produced along the same lines as port wine. The Grenache grape is an ingredient in both Banyul and Maury, and gives an attractive fruitiness and smoothness, but which develops its chocolate, caramel and blood orange nuances during storage. Chocolate buffs often wax lyrical over Banyul wines in particular.

The above wines are my personal favorites to go with bittersweet desserts, and are often the favorites at the many wine and chocolate tastings I have lead. But what of the many wines and light dessert wines that are not fortified with liquor? A bottle of Recioto della Valpolicella, if you can find one, is a sweet amarone variety, and is well suited to less sweet chocolate desserts. Sacher Torte, for example, can be served with a full-bodied golden dessert wine such as trockenbeerenauslese (whatever kind of grape it is made of). These are basically the same as Sauternes, that is, made from grapes that have been infected with botrytis mold, but are much sweeter, more full-bodied and well rounded. This combination of tropical fruit (to be found in all wines of this sort) and the apricot in the Sacher Torte is particularly successful. The wines are also extremely sweet, and taste sufficiently full-bodied to parry the powerful chocolate flavor.

Moscato Rosa, or a sweet, sparkling red wine such as Brachetto d'Acqui, from northern Italy, are exciting wines that are often forgotten in this context.

Light dessert wines can be served to their advantage with light chocolate desserts, truffles, mousse or ice cream. If tropical fruit, sauces or sweetened fruit salads dominate, they can best be paired with a wine with similar aromas. Sauternes, and similar wines from Bordeaux, are, however, never successful since they are not sweet enough and have a too pronounced tannin taste (partly from the oak barrels).

And what about liquor?

Liquor and chocolate is a much appreciated topic of conversation, but liquor is usually preferred with chocolate liqueurs and petits fours rather than with the dessert itself. The ground rules for liquor are somewhat different than for wine. Liqueurs apart, most liquor is dry, and far less sweet than the dessert. So, you make use of aroma when composing an encounter between the two. Try to ensure that the aroma of the liquor is matched by similar aromas in the chocolate. Aromas such as white raisin, caramel, vanilla, burnt sugar, nougat, nuts and prunes and, of course, the chocolate in itself, can all be found in high-class vintage oak-matured liquor. A fully matured cognac or armagnac (preferably XO or Extra) is better than younger grape distillates, which are usually felt to be too strong and fiery. This kind of liquor always lacks the body and smoothness that can only be achieved by long storage. Spanish brandy is also excellent, both cheaper and more rounded since it is often sweetened with fortified wine or plum extract before bottling. Vintage West Indian, oak-matured rum can add yet another dimension thanks to its discrete caramel sweetness, its undertones of vanilla and whisky barrels, its delicious aroma of arrack.

Let a dark chocolate truffle, flavored with vanilla and an elegant liquor, melt on the tongue while you sip cognac, armagnac or rum—that's what I call quality of life! Complementary gastronomic hard currency. What more could you possibly want?

I don't want to leave out liqueurs either. They contain at least 1 oz sugar per 10 fl oz and are therefore often used to round off a meal. But I think you can also use them in the dessert itself. The ground rules are more or less the same as for liquor. Proceed from what I have already mentioned but try to find a taste combination in the liqueur similar to your dessert, such as citrus fruits, pear or raspberry. A Cointreau (citrus liqueur) is excellent with chocolate mousse, a Poire au Cognac (cognac marinated pear) tastes well with a chocolate muffin or a Crème de Framboise (raspberry liqueur) is an exciting choice for a bittersweet chocolate truffle. However, neither a Kloster liqueur, which is too bitter, spicy and complex, nor a cream liqueur, which is too fatty and creamy, are particularly suited to chocolate.

Clear fruit distillates, or eau de vie de fruits, fill the same aromatic role as the liqueurs but are less sweet. Try one of the different German or Alsace varieties, or why not Swedish schnapps flavored with Seville orange (Årsta brännvinn or Rånäs brännvin) or black currant. Certainly different, decidedly good and definitely memorable!

Beer and chocolate?!

"Port—are you mad? Chocolate tastes best with a foaming stout," was the advice an old gentleman gave when I was just starting out as a sommelier. And he was right, of course! Slightly roasted, and with similar aromas to chocolate, a stout beer is often an excellent complement to chocolate. Other types of beer, excepting lagers and English bitters, can also be worth a try. The strong Belgian abbey beers are based on sweet malt and are often delightfully flavored with Seville orange and spices. Other possible beers are a very strong, full-bodied barley wine or imperial stout. Both are made from dark roasted malt and have a caramel sweetness without being openly sweet. You will probably notice that the beer often seems drier and a little raw in its encounter with chocolate, but see it as an exciting meeting of aromas and not a fight.

These types of beer are most suited to bittersweet or semisweet chocolate puddings, sticky chocolate cake or small delicious truffles.

Advice on serving...

Now that we've arrived at the blissful moment when this sweet nectar is due to be tasted with the chocolate, I'd like to give you a last few words of advice. You may serve the wine or beer chilled but never cold, for this dampens the finest aromas. A couple of degrees above refrigerator temperature, 55°F, is perfect for beer and light dessert wines, while darker, fortified wines should be 55–65°F. Liqueur should be slightly chilled, but other liquor should be more or less at room temperature.

Choosing the right glass is also very important. Pouring a beautiful, sweet dessert wine into a tiny liqueur or sherry glass is a waste. And for liquor in general I would prefer to smash all the so-called cognac balloons and replace them with small bulb glasses, which are infinitely superior for aroma and taste. For all kinds of wine you should use proper wine glasses with a good bowl, but do not pour too much wine in the glass. This is the best, in fact only, way that the aroma can flower—something that should be a matter of course for all wines.

Savor, relish, relax and enjoy life!

Michel Jamais
Sommelier and chocolate freak

Index